Money

The **Vocabulary** of
the Financial World

SECOND EDITION

Raymond C. Clark

Pro Lingua Associates

Pro Lingua Associates, Publishers
74 Cotton Mill Hill, Suite A315
Brattleboro, Vermont 05302 USA
Office: 802-257-7779
Orders: 800-366- 4775
Email: info@ProLinguaAssociates.com
WebStore www.ProLinguaAssociates.com
SAN: 216-0579

At Pro Lingua
our objective is to foster an approach
to learning and teaching that we call
interplay, *the* **inter***action of language*
learners and teachers with their materials,
with the language and culture,
and with each other in active, creative,
and productive **play**.

Text ISBN 978-0-86647-483-2
Audio CD ISBN 978-0-86647-484-9
Text/CD set ISBN 978-0-86647-485-6
Digital Edition ISBN 978-0-86647-486-3

Money: The Vocabulary of the Financial World was designed by Arthur A. Burrows. It was set in Palatino, the most widely used, and pirated, face of the twentieth century, which was designed by Hermann Zapf in 1948 in Frankfurt. Although modern, it is based on Renaissance designs typical of the Palatinate area in Germany.

Photo Credits: Front cover © xx/Dreamstime; back cover @ xx/Dreamstime; red leather © Banprick/ Dreamstime; title page © Candy 1812/Dreamstime.com. The following illustrations are from Dreamstime.com: halftitle page xi © Roman Romaniuk; p xii © StellarStock & © Chakis Thurankorn; p 4 © Oleksandr Zheltobriukh; p 5 © Alexandersikov; p 9 © Mauricio Jordan De Souza Coelho; p 10 © Lakesphotostudio; p 14 © Robert Kneschke; p. 15 © Duard Van Der Westhuizen; p 18 © Hongqi Zhang (aka Michael Zhang) ; p 22 © Jill Battaglia & © Yukchong Kwan; p 23 © Adamgregor; p 26 © Maxuser; p 31 © Ivansmuk; p 35 © Robert Bleile; p 39 © Rawpixelimages; p 42 © Orensila; p 46 © Cheryl Quigley; p 49 © Julián Rovagnati; p 51 © Keechuan; p. 55 © Tang90246; p 56 © Alexandr Bazhanov; p 60 © Rawpixelimages; p 64 © Aprescindere; p 68 © Spectruminfo; p 75 © Oleksandr Zheltobriukh.

The book was printed and bound by King Printing Co., Inc. in Lowell, Massachusetts.

Printed in the United States of America
Second Edition, first printing 2019.

Introduction

The purpose of this book is to help learners of English develop their vocabulary in an efficient and enjoyable way. It is part of a series of vocabulary texts published by Pro Lingua since 1984.*

As is obvious, the key words all relate to a lexical field: the world of finance, or more simply, money. This grouping of words allows the learner to focus on words that in one way or another, connect with each other. This interconnectedness allows the learner to develop their vocabulary systematically rather than randomly.

The recommended proficiency level is low intermediate with a basic vocabulary of about 600 words. Age level: high school and up.

* See the list of books on the last page of this book.

Acknowledgements

I would like to thank the many people who helped me, directly and indirectly, in the writing and preparation of this material.

The first edition was written for intermediate-level English language students at the Center for International Banking Studies (CIBS) in Istanbul, Turkey. I would like to acknowledge the support of the staff of the Center. Special thanks are due to Aslam Aziz and Lee Sherrill, banking course directors at CIBS. They helped me understand the vocabulary of banking and finance.

The English program at CIBS was a program of The School for International Training, Brattleboro, Vermont. My SIT colleagues in Istanbul were Janie Duncan, Daryl Newton, Kathleen Quinby, Andy Reyes, and Melinda Taplin. Along with them I learned and taught a lot of "Financial English," and I have put some of that knowledge to use in the preparation of this material. A special thank you to Janie Duncan, who helped write some of the exercises.

Finally, I am grateful for the assistance of Nazli Kiral, who typed the original manuscript, and for the assistance of Andy Burrows and Jonathan Clark.
– RCC, Istanbul, 1988

For this second edition, I would again like to thank Andy Burrows and Janie Duncan for their review of the new material.
– RCC, Brattleboro, 2018

Contents

1 Introductory Reading 🏛 1

___ needs	___ services	___ luxury	___ economic
___ earn	___ useful	___ use	___ the economy
___ goods	___ necessity	___ economics	___ economist

2 Money: A Short History 🏛 3

___ coin	___ commodity	___ payment	___ value
___ bill	___ worth	___ transaction	___ cash
___ currency	___ precious	___ mint	___ supply

3 Using Money 🏛 8

___ exchange	___ spend	___ purchase	___ loan
___ counterfeit	___ invest	___ borrow	___ collect
___ save	___ interest	___ lend	___ gamble

4 Earning Money 🏛 13

___ income	___ wages	___ raise	___ consultant
___ royalties	___ salary	___ bonus	___ wealth
___ employ	___ contract	___ fee	___ capital

5 Buying and Selling 🏛 18

___ production	___ wholesale	___ dealer	___ promotion
___ distribution	___ retail	___ marketing	___ bargain
___ profit	___ consumer	___ competition	___ offer
			___ bid

6 Banks 🏛 22

___ financial	___ deposit	___ draw	___ funds
___ commercial	___ withdraw	___ statement	___ minimum
___ trade	___ balance	___ bounce	___ reserve

⛫ CONTENTS ⛫

User's Guide

This second edition of *Money* is a photocopyable teacher's resource. As such, it can be used in a number of ways, adapted as necessary to fit your teaching situation and your students. It can, of course, be used as a student text, with each student having a copy of the book. Used as a teacher resource, the basic procedure would be to use selected units on an occasional basis, once or twice a week with ongoing follow-up reviews. It is suggested that you start with the first unit, "An Introductory Reading" to introduce the learners to the format of the book.

An optional audio component with all of the readings is available to supplement the text. It can be used to introduce the unit or follow up on the reading or even as an audio book for self-study.

Additional follow-up information is available in the Appendices.

A basic procedure:

1. Introduce the book with the first unit, *An Introductory Reading*. You can give the learners the *Learner's Guide* on the following pages.

2. List the key words on the board or as a separate handout. See the table of contents for the words that will be the focus of the lesson.

3. Explore the meanings of the key words. Have the learners work in small groups to see if they know the meanings of the words.

- Give them five minutes to work together.
- Have each group report on what they know and do not know.
- Focus on the "Don't Know" words and tell them to look for them in the reading.

4. For the very first unit, you read the passage aloud. This keeps everyone "on the same page." You can stop or pause as you encounter each key word, but it is usually more effective to read the entire passage through without stopping.

5. Have the learners look at the key words at the end of the reading. Continue to explore the meaning of the key words.

6. Have the learners do the exercises in class or assign them as homework. If you do the exercises in class, as learners finish, pair them to compare each other's answers.

7. Hand out and go over the answers.

8. After completing the reading and the exercises, do the *Talk About It* questions using the key words and concepts in conversation.

9. As you proceed through the book, recycle the fourth exercise from previous units.

Appendices: Additional information in the appendices may be used simply as interesting information or as conversation prompts.

Answers: The answers for the exercises are available for copying for the the students.

Key Word Index: This is an alphabetical list of all the key words with the number of the unit in which each appears.

Learner's Guide

This book is a vocabulary development text that focuses on words about money. There are 200 key words; the form, meaning, and usage of these key words is explored in the exercises that follow the reading.

The key words are presented in sixteen readings. The passages are written in a way that will help you learn the meaning of each key word through the context – the thoughts that precede and follow the word. Although you may have to use a dictionary from time to time, you should first try to understand the words by studying the context. By doing this, you will also develop your reading skills.

The units are organized according to the following plan:

Reading: Each reading is a description of some aspect of using money. The key vocabulary is in **bold** type.

Exercises: There are four exercises after each reading so you can practice using each key word and its forms (noun, verb, adjective).

Talk About It: After completing the reading and exercises, use the words in conversation.

Money

The Vocabulary of
the
Financial World

1
An Introductory Reading

Basic human physical **needs** are food, shelter, and clothing, but in today's world we need money to get food, shelter, and clothing. To get money, we **earn** it by making **goods** or providing **services** that are necessary, **useful**, and enjoyable. Some goods, such as food and clothing, are **necessities**; some goods, such as jewelry, are **luxuries**. Services are different from goods; one person does something for another person. Teaching, for example, is a service.

We **use** money every day. We use it in different forms, such as coins, bills, checks, and credit or debit cards, and we do many different things with our money – buying, saving, and borrowing, for example. All of the things we do with money can be called economic activity. **Economics** is the science of studying this activity. The **economic** system is called **the economy**, and a person who studies all this is an **economist**.

The organizations at the center of all this activity are banks. We use banks for many purposes, and banks use money for many purposes, but the basic purpose of most banks is to earn money.

Exercises

A. In each of the following sentences, fill in the blank with one of the key words. Use each word only once.

1. For most of us, beautiful, expensive clothes are a _____ , but for all of us, clothes are a _____ .

2. Things such as clothes, books, and machines are _____ , and activities such as teaching, selling goods, and changing money are _____.

3. Most people carry money with them because they need to _____ it every day.

4. Banks provide a _____ service.

5. He teaches _____ , and he explains _____ theory. He is an _____.

6. His _____ are very simple: food, fire, and friends.

7. She _____ a lot of money by selling clothes.

8. _____ _____ is very good right now.

B. Fill in the blanks with the appropriate words, as in this example: A person who teaches is a ***teacher.***

1. A person who works in a bank is a _____.

2. A person who buys things is a _____.

3. A person who sells things is a _____.

4. A person who uses things is a _____.

5. A person who earns things is an _____.

6. A person who borrows is a _____.

7. But a person who studies economics is an _____.

Talk About It

1. What are your necessities and luxuries?
2. Do you work with goods or services?
3. Do you have a bank account? What kind?
4. Have you studied economics? Did you like it?

Money: A Short History

Money, as we know it today, comes in two physical forms: **coins** and **bills**, also called **currency**. Coins are made from metal, and bills are made from paper. Sometimes bills are called paper money. But, as we shall see later, money also exists in another way, such as in the form of bank deposits and cryptocurrencies.

In earlier days, and even today in some isolated parts of the world, people developed a form of money called **commodity** money. This was the use of things that by themselves have some value or importance and can be used as a standard measure of exchange. For example, one cow might be **worth** twenty bags of rice or thirty chickens. Some examples of this kind of money are seashells in New Guinea, rice in Japan, and iron bars in Nigeria.

Little by little, people began to use **precious** metals as a convenient form of commodity money, and gold, silver, and copper eventually became the most commonly used metals. They were useful because they could be carried, they could be split into smaller sizes, and, perhaps because of their beauty, they were acceptable as **payment** for something in many different places. But there were disadvantages. They could be debased (base metals such as lead and tin could be added to decrease the purity), and it was necessary to weigh the metal each time a **transaction** was made and people exchanged the precious metal for goods or services.

The solution was to **mint** coins from the metal. To show and guarantee the value of the coin, symbols of national authority, such as the head of the king, were stamped on the coins. The use of coinage goes back over 2,500 years, to the Lydians of Anatolia (now Turkey), and the use of coins in international trade goes back at least to the time of Alexander the Great. All of these early coins shared one feature - the **value** of the coin was based on the amount of precious metal that it contained.

Ancient Greek: Alexander and Philip II

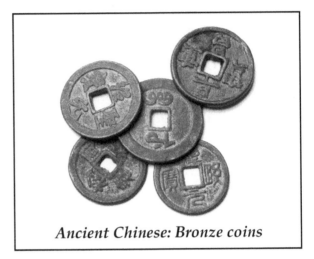

Ancient Chinese: Bronze coins

During the seventeenth century, bank notes first came into use as currency, the beginning of an important development. At first the bank note was a promise to pay in coin, but the note itself had no actual value. The value of the note was tied to precious metal. This is no longer true, but until early in the twentieth century almost all currencies were tied to gold or silver.

The final step in the development of money was reached in the twentieth century when we began to think of bank deposits (the amount we have in our checkbooks and savings books) as the same as the **cash** that we carry in our pockets, purses, and wallets. In fact, in today's world the major part of the world's **supply** of money does not exist as coins and bills but only as numbers on the books of the world's banks. For this reason, it is possible to say that most of the world's money does not exist.

Currencies of the Future?

Nowadays a new kind of currency is becoming known and used. The name for the currency is cryptocurrency.* There are several different cryptocurrencies, but the best-known and most widely used is the bitcoin. These currencies are significantly different from physical cash or gold or numbers in bank accounts. For one thing, the units, like the bitcoin, are not in any bank or under the control of any government. Essentially, a transaction with a cryptocurrency is between two "peers." For example, if I want to buy or sell something to someone else, it is almost as if the payment is made from one person's hand directly to another person's hand. The two peers may be in two different rooms in the same building or on two different continents. To learn more about this new thing, look at the website below:

https://blockgeeks.com/guides/what-is-cryptocurrency/
also: https://en.wikipedia.org/wiki/Crypto

* Crypto is from Greek, meaning "secret" or "hidden."

coins	commodity	payment	value
bills	worth	transaction	cash
currency	precious	minted	supply

Exercises

A. Underline the correct form of the key word.

1. This jewelry is very (value, valued, valuable).
2. That country (supplies, supply, supplying) the world with many valuable (commodities, commodity).
3. (Cash, Cashed, Cashing) a check is a common (transactional, transaction, transacted) at a bank.
4. Tin is not a (preciously, precious) metal.
5. How much is the Euro (worthless, worthwhile, worth)?
6. The (coined, coining, coinage) of the U.S. includes pennies, nickels, dimes, quarters, and half-dollars; the common (bill, bills, billings) include the one-, two-, five-, ten-, and twenty-dollar bank notes.
7. The dollar also is the basic unit of the (currencies, current, currently) of Canada, Australia, and New Zealand.
8. Will you accept a check in (pay, payment, paying) for these things?
9. The place where coins are (mints, minting, minted) is called a (mint, minter, minting).

B. Use the key words above in the following sentences. Use each word only once.

1. This coin is not _____ a lot of money. In fact, it is almost worthless.
2. In addition to gold and silver, platinum is also a _____ metal.
3. _____are not made out of paper, but _____are.
4. He never carries _____ with him.
5. Rice is a _____.
6. The _____ of China, the yuan, has increased in _____ in recent years.
7. The act of buying and selling something can be called a business _____.
8. The company is expecting to receive _____ for its services within 30 days.
9. The government has never _____ a two-dollar coin.
10. Is the world's money _____ constantly increasing?

C. Use the correct form of the key word in parentheses.

1. (value) She has a lot of _____ jewelry. Its _____ is probably more than $10,000.
2. (worth) This coin has no value; it is _____.
3. (mint, supply) The U.S. _____ has _____ us with our coins.
4. (commodity) Gold and silver are _____.
5. (payment) They will _____ for their car in monthly _____.
6. (transaction) His new company _____ a lot of business in the first few days of this month. The very first _____ involved thousands of pounds.
7. (cash) I needed some _____, so I _____ a check.

D. Use a key word in each of these sentences.

1. Can you change a twenty-dollar _____?
2. This coin has just come from the mint; it's in _____ condition.
3. This land is still_____ a lot of money, but its _____ has decreased a little since last year.
4. _____stones, such as diamonds, can be very expensive.
5. The _____market includes food, livestock, and metals.
6. They will accept only _____ in _____ for their product.
7. In the_____ market people buy and sell _____ such as dollars, euros, yen, and pounds.
8. You'll need a _____ to use a public vending machine; it's _____-operated.
9. The act of putting money in a bank can be called a _____.
10. Saudi Arabia is an important _____of oil. It _____ much of the oil consumed in Europe.

Talk About It

1. Should the US stop printing the dollar bill and replace it with a dollar coin?
2. Will it be easy to change to a dollar coin?
3. What about the one-cent coin (penny)? Is it worthless? Why do some people want to keep it?

3

Using Money

In simple terms we receive money for our work, and we **exchange** this money for things that we need or want. The money comes in to us, and the money goes out to somebody else who then exchanges it for something they need, and so on. Money, then, is actually a medium of exchange that enables people to exchange goods and services in a convenient and efficient way. Money is like the oil and grease that we use to keep the great economic machine working.

The most common way in which people get money is to earn it by working, and although we often use the phrase "make money" to mean "earn it," in fact we do not actually mint coins or print bills. Only **counterfeiters** print their own money, illegally.

Let's look at what happens after we are paid for our work. Basically, we have a choice, we can **save** our money or **spend** it on something. The decisions that each individual person makes on saving and spending, when taken together with everybody else's decisions, can have a major effect on the economy.

If we decide to save our money, there are several ways in which we can save. We can simply keep our money in a safe place, just as a child may keep coins in a "piggy bank." But money saved in this way can actually lose value if prices rise while the money is sitting in a safe place. Another way to save money is to **invest** it, which means that we let somebody else use the money and they pay us **interest**. In this way, our savings earn money.

If a person prefers or needs to use their money, they probably will buy something, let's say food, from somebody else. The thing that is bought is called a **purchase**. Buying and selling are two very basic activities in the world of business. The businessperson's goal is to make money, just like anybody else who works, but occasionally a businessperson who spends more on their business than they earn will lose money.

Another activity that is familiar to all of us is **borrowing** and **lending**. On a personal level, people often borrow money from each other for a short time (and sometimes forget to repay it). And in the world of business, making **loans** (lending money) is one of the main activities of a bank.

1890 Morgan Silver Dollar: A highly valued collectible.

Finally, we should mention two other activities associated with money. Some people like to **collect** money, especially coins, and sometimes a good coin collection can be a good investment. Other people like to **gamble** with their money by buying lottery tickets, going to horse races, or spending time and money in gambling casinos in places like Monaco and Las Vegas.

<table>
<tr><td colspan="4" align="center">*Key words*</td></tr>
<tr><td>exchanges</td><td>spent</td><td>purchase</td><td>loan</td></tr>
<tr><td>counterfeit</td><td>investment</td><td>borrow</td><td>collection</td></tr>
<tr><td>save</td><td>interest</td><td>lend</td><td>gamble</td></tr>
</table>

Exercises

A. Underline the correct form of the key word.

1. How much did you (spend, spending, spent) on food last week?
2. Would you (lend, lending, lent) me some money?
3. A bank makes money by (loans, loaned, loaning) it.
4. Have you ever (borrow, borrowing, borrowed) money from a bank?
5. After she had (saved, saving, saves) a lot of money, she (purchases, purchased, purchase) a new car.
6. My friend (investment, invests, invest) in bonds and makes over $500 a month in (interests, interest, interesting).
7. (Gamble, Gambling, Gambler) is very exciting for the (gamble, gambling, gambler), just as (collecting, collects, collection) money is exciting for the (collection, collector, collecting).
8. (Counterfeits, Counterfeiting, Counterfeiter) is illegal.
9. Workers (exchange, exchanging, exchanges) work for money.

B. Use the key words in the following sentences. Use each word only once.

1. I _____ all my money on clothes, so now I need a _____. Can I _____ $20.00 from you? If you'll _____ me the money, I'll give you _____ .
2. The worker _____ his labor for money. He uses it to _____ goods. He may _____ some of it in a _____ account.
3. I don't think this property is a good _____ , but if you like to _____ , you could take a chance. Its value might increase.
4. He thought his coin_____ was very valuable, until he discovered that the "Spanish doubloons" were all _____ and therefore worthless.

C. Use the correct form of the key word in parentheses.

1. (loan) My parents _____ me the money for my new car.
2. (borrow) I also _____ some money from my grandmother.
3. (interest) Naturally, they didn't charge me any _____ .
4. (purchase) I actually _____ the car last week.
5. (spend) I _____ some more money on the registration and insurance.
6. (counterfeit) The police finally caught the _____ .
7. (collect) Another word for a coin _____ is a numismatist, a person who _____ coins.
8. (gamble, save) I don't like to _____ ; I would rather put my money into a _____ account.
9. (invest) He _____ all his money in that company, and lost it all.
10. (exchange) The basis of business is the _____ of goods or services for money.

D. Use a key word in each of these sentences.

1. I _____ stamps and coins. Would you _____ some stamps for me so I can add them to my _____ ?
2. Can I _____ this shirt for another one that is smaller?
3. The police caught the _____ as he was trying to _____ his "funny money" at my store.
4. My father is going to _____ in some land. He thinks it will be a good _____ . But first, he needs to get a _____ from a bank.
5. Right now, my savings account is paying 1.5% _____ .
6. Drinking alcohol and driving a car is not only against the law. It is _____ with your life.

Talk About It

How do you use money? Use these words: save, spend, purchase, invest, borrow, lend, loan, collect, gamble.

4
Earning Money

When people work they produce something, and what they produce has value. In today's complex world, it is not always easy to understand how one kind of work has greater value than another kind of work. For example, a farmer produces food, which everyone needs, and a rock star produces music, which is not usually considered a need. But the difference between the **income** of the farmer and the rock star is huge. Of course, there are many reasons why there is such a difference. The farmer's production is somewhat limited, and even though the owner of a large farm may produce enough food to feed several thousand people, a rock star's hit song may be sold to millions of people, and the star's **royalties** from these sales may amount to millions of dollars. Rock stars can become millionaires. Farmers rarely do.

Another difference between the rock star and the farmer is that the farmer produces goods while the rock musician provides a service. Most of the world's jobs can be classified in this way. In general, complex societies have more people working in services.

Another way in which **employment** can be characterized is by its workforce. In general, "blue-collar" workers work with their hands and are paid hourly **wages**. "White-collar" workers work with their heads and are paid an annual **salary**. However, they are both paid on a regular basis (weekly, bi-weekly, monthly), usually with a paycheck. Payday, whether weekly or bi-weekly, is an important day. In one other way, there is a difference: white-collar employees often have a **contract** with their employer. The contract is an agreement that sometimes protects the employee for certain periods of time

Blue-collar workers doing industrial work.

and guarantees a certain salary. Blue-collar workers, on the other hand, may not have a personal contract with their employer, but they belong to a union which has a contract with the employer. When it is time for a new **contract**, the union may ask for a **raise** in pay so that the workers will get more money. Some employers give their employees a **bonus**, a special payment for doing something very well.

Some kinds of professional people, for example doctors and lawyers, receive **fees** for their services. Some experts who work for short periods of time for very specific jobs, such as building a bridge or advising a business or a government, are called **consultants**, and they may receive a one-time payment. Sometimes they are paid a lot of money, and sometimes they are given a small gift called an honorarium.

White-collar workers planning a project.

Then there are a few people who don't need to work, because they already have a great deal of **wealth**. Some of them continue to work to earn more, while others have never worked or are retired. In any case, their wealth works for them. They may have their money invested in banks or in the stock market, or they may have their money invested in the ownership of property; both forms of wealth are called **capital**. And this is the origin of the well-known label, capitalist. A capitalist is anyone whose wealth (capital) is invested to earn them more money.

Key words			
income	wages	raise	consultant
royalties	salary	bonus	wealthy
employed	contract	fee	capital

Exercises

A. Underline the correct form of the key word.

1. "You're a (capital, capitalist, capitalistic)," he shouted.
2. The royal family is extremely (wealth, wealthy).
3. The athlete has refused to sign a (contract, contracted, contractual) with his team.
4. Their expenses are greater than their (income, incoming).
5. She collects (royalty, royalties, royal) checks from several different recording companies.
6. Although prices have gone up, (wage, waged, wages) have not.
7. The company gave all its (employer, employees, employment) a (salary, salaried, salaries) increase.
8. All his earnings this year came from (fee, fees, feed).
9. Let's (consulting, consult, consultant) with an expert on this problem.
10. Not all of the employees got (raise, raised, raises) this year.
11. Only a few people got (bonus, bonuses) this year.

B. Use the key words above in the following sentences. Use each word only once.

1. The singer's income from _____ is more than $500,000 a year. He must be a millionaire by now.
2. The workers want a new _____ with the owners.
3. The lawyer's _____ for his services is $500.
4. The employees' daily _____ have not increased.
5. She is paid an annual _____; her _____ is over $30,000 a year.
6. Any business needs _____ in order to operate.
7. As a _____, he earned an honorarium of $3,000 for his services.
8. I'm not _____; I don't have a lot of money.
9. She has been_____ by that company for ten years.
10. I've got to ask for a _____; I'm not making enough money.
11. On January 1, all the employees got a New Year's _____ because the company did very well during the previous year.

C. Use the correct form of the key word in parentheses.

1. (salary) The cost of living has gone up, but our _____ haven't.
2. (wage) The minimum _____ in this state is $ 7.25 an hour.
3. (wealth, income) Although he is extremely _____ , he didn't pay any _____ tax last year.
4. (consult) We need an expert. Let's get a _____.
5. (employ) After three months of unemployment, he was happy to be _____ again.
6. (royalty) She gets a 20% _____ on all her books.
7. (bonus, raise) Both of them got _____ and _____ .
8. (fee) Yes, he's a good doctor, but his _____ are very high.
9. (capital) We have studied socialism and _____ .

D. Use a key word in each of these sentences.

1. Her company _____ over 500 people.
2. _____ is the actual property and investments of a business.
3. The managers all got a 10% _____ increase.
4. The hourly _____ rate is $15.50.
5. His wife still receives the _____ from the book he wrote.
6. As a highly paid _____ , he needs to work only a few months each year.
7. The bank will charge a small _____ for this service.
8. The union is asking for a 10% pay _____.
9. The football player signed a _____ with the Giants.
10. Most states have a state_____ tax.
11. Early to bed and early to rise keeps one healthy, _____ , and wise.
12. Something extra that we don't expect to receive is a _____.

Talk About It

1. What is a "good" salary in these times?
2. What kind of work is overpaid or underpaid?
3. What are your salary goals?

5

Buying and Selling

Many people use currency for ordinary, everyday buying or selling, although more and more people use checks and credit cards. Buying and selling is the basis for the world of business. A simple description of business is the **production, distribution**, and sale of goods and services for a **profit**. In other words, business is based on selling the product at a price that is higher than the cost of making and delivering the product or goods.

There are two kinds of sales: **wholesale** and **retail**. In wholesale trade, a producer sells large quantities of his product to retailers (store owners, for example) and the retailers sell the product in smaller amounts to individual **consumers**. In the auto industry, for example, the manufacturer of the car sells it wholesale to a retailer (called a **dealer** in the auto industry) who in turn charges a higher price and sells the car to a customer. Both the wholesaler and the retailer hope to make a profit from their transactions.

A very important part of contemporary business is **marketing**. Marketing is important because businesses are in **competition** with each other to sell their products to customers. It is obvious that it is important to get and maintain a market share that will allow a company to be competitive and make a profit. Marketing influences the entire business cycle from production to sales, and in recent years the **promotion** of the product, especially in advertisements, has become a very important operation.

In the final act, when buyer and seller are face to face, most sales are based on a fixed price. However, some transactions, especially those for very expensive items such as houses and automobiles, are done through **bargaining**, in which the buyer can make an **offer** that is below the asking price. Sometimes in private sales, where an individual might be selling a used refrigerator, the buyer and seller may also bargain.

In another kind of sales transaction, especially when a government is purchasing goods or services, the buyer asks for competitive **bids**, and several suppliers each make a bid for a contract to supply the goods or services. The lowest bidder, of course, gets the contract. In a somewhat similar situation, a person or business may sell something by auction. In an auction, the seller asks buyers to make a bid, and the highest bid gets the product, as the auctioneer says "going, going, gone!" which means the sale is completed.

Key words

production	wholesale	dealer	promotion	bid
distribution	retail	marketing	bargain	
profit	consumer	competitors	offer	

Exercises

A. Underline the correct form of the key word.

1. What a (deal, dealt, dealing)! I bought the refrigerator at almost (wholesale, wholesaling), and I didn't even (bargaining, bargain, bargained).
2. In order to (market, marketing, marketable) our product in Tokyo, we need to (promotion, promote, promoter) it on TV.
3. Their new (production, product, producer) is priced way below ours. How can we (competitive, competition, compete) with them?
4. The government report says that retail sales have increased in the last few months. This has made (retailers, retailing, retail) very happy. Their (profiting, profiteers, profits) will be higher.
5. We have a new (distribution, distributor) for the West Coast market.
6. That's a beautiful chair. Let's make an (offering, offer). Shall we (bid, bidding) $25?
7. How much did you (spend, spending, spent) on food last week?

B. Use the key words above in the following sentences. Use each word only once.

1. Consumers have not been spending; therefore _____ sales are down.
2. A _____ buys cars at _____ and sells them to _____ at retail.
3. We need to make a 20% _____ if we're going to stay in business, but our _____ are selling their product at a very low price.
4. Machines are used in the _____ of goods.
   Vehicles are used in the _____ of goods.
   Advertisements are used in the _____ of products.
5. The price is $5,000, but I'm going to _____ $4,500.
6. At an auction, the highest_____ wins.
7. Our new _____ manager wants to change the name of our product and advertise it on TV.
8. If you buy something at a very low price, you can say you got a _____.

C. Give the correct form of the word. Be sure to check your answers for the correct spelling.

1. A person who consumes is a _____.
2. A person who bids is a _____. (Watch the spelling!)
3. A person who deals is a _____.
4. A person in distribution is a _____.
5. A person in promotion is a _____.
6. A person who makes an offer is an _____.
7. A person in production is a _____.
8. A person in wholesale trade is a _____.
9. A person in retail trade is a _____ .
10. A person involved in _____ is a competitor.
11. A person who makes a very high _____ can be called a profiteer.

D. Use a key word in each of these sentences.

1. How much will you _____ for this Turkish carpet?
2. When you're in Boston, be sure to visit Quincy _____ ; it's a great place to shop.
3. General Motors has_____ millions of automobiles.
4. Athletes from all over the world will be_____ in the Olympics.
5. They under-_____ us and got the contract.
6. We can say that a person who learns from his mistakes, _____ from them.
7. The average _____ buys twenty-four bars of soap every year.
8. In a card game, the person who takes and gives the cards is called the _____.
9. The post office is involved in the _____ of mail.
10. She spent two days _____ for the car, and finally bought it for $25,000. I think she got a real _____.
11. Advertising is one form of _____. The verb to _____ can also mean "to give a higher position." For example, he was _____ to Vice President.

Talk About It
1. Do you prefer to buy or sell?
2. Would you be more interested in retail or wholesale?
3. What kinds of things would you enjoy selling?
4. Are you interested in marketing?

6
Banks

For most of us, the most important and best-known **financial** institution is our local bank. Probably our bank is a **commercial** bank, meaning that the bank is involved in **trade**, and what it trades in is money and other financial services. It carries out this trade for a profit, just as any business does.

A bank carries out a variety of functions. For its customers it operates savings and checking accounts; it offers loans; it changes money. With the familiar savings account, the customer can save money and earn interest. The customer deposits and withdraws money, and his **deposits** and **withdrawals**, along with his interest earnings and the **balance** (the total of deposits minus withdrawals), are recorded in a passbook.

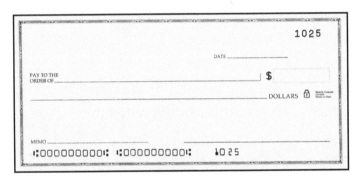

check

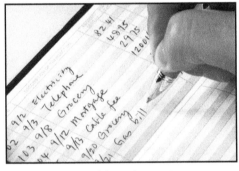

checkbook register

A checking account is a service that usually makes our lives a little easier. The bank holds our money and we pay our bills by writing checks instead of using cash – checks **drawing** on our accounts. We record each check we write in a check register in our checkbook. The checks come back to our bank through a clearinghouse, and our accounts are charged for the checks we have written. At the end of each month we receive a **statement** which summarizes our transactions. Then we compare the bank statement with our check register.

Although checking accounts are very helpful, we can sometimes make problems for ourselves by **bouncing** a check. The check bounces back to us like a ball (a check that bounces is called a rubber check). It is marked "insufficient **funds**," meaning we do not have enough money in our account to cover the check; we have overdrawn our account.

Banks usually have a service charge for maintaining our checking accounts, although some banks do not charge us if we keep a **minimum** balance in our account. So for example, if the minimum is $500 and our balance never goes below $500, we do not pay a service charge.

In recent years people have been using debit cards more than checks. The debit card can be used to make payments, like a credit card, but the money is automatically withdrawn from the checking account.

In addition to operating accounts, banks also loan money and charge interest on the loans. Although banks always try to keep a certain amount of money in **reserve** to cover withdrawals, they invest a large part of the money they are holding to earn more money. They also offer other services for a fee, such as storing valuables for people in safe deposit boxes inside the bank's vault and changing currencies.

In short, banks provide services and use our money to make money.

Exercises

A. Underline the correct form of the key word.

1. Did you (bounce, bounced, bouncing) a check this month?
2. We don't have enough (fund, funds, funded) in our account.
3. Wall Street is the (financing, financial, financed) center of the U.S.
4. The bank is required to keep a certain amount of money in (reservation, reserving, reserve).
5. We can get interest if our (balancing, balance, balanced) is above the (minimum, minimal).
6. This month my (deposit, deposits, depositing) were greater than my (withdraws, withdrawals).
7. (Commerce, Commercials) is another word for trade.
8. She works on the stock exchange as a (trade, trading, trader). She probably (draws, draw, drawing) a large salary.

B. Use the key words in the sentences below. Use each key word only once.

1. I'm trying to save money, so I _____ $20 a week in my savings account.
2. I need some money, so I'll_____ $20 from my account.
3. I'm not going to use all my money right now, so I'll keep some in _____.
4. I want to _____ a check on my account in the First National Bank.
5. I received my bank _____ this week, and it shows that I have a _____ of $525. That's only $25 above the _____ balance for the special checking account.
6. A sum or supply of money can be called _____.
7. Another word for exchange is _____.
8. A _____ bank hopes to make a profit.
9. The _____ Times is a newspaper that is read by economists, bankers, and business people.
10. He wrote me a bad check; it _____.

C. Use the correct form of the key word in parentheses.

    1. (reserve) Our cash _____ are getting low.

    2. (deposit) She_____ the check yesterday,

    3. (withdraw) and then she made a _____.

    4. (balance) Then she _____ her checkbook,

    5. (minimum) and discovered that her balance was below the _____.

    6. (statement) There will be a service charge on her next _____.

    7. (draw) A bank draft is used to _____ on an account.

    8. (fund) The World Bank _____ development in Third World countries.

    9. (trade) Last week he _____ his old Cadillac for a new ZX3.

    10. (finance) He was a _____ success at the age of thirty-two.

    11. (commerce) The _____ center of the city is near the river.

    12. (bounce) Until yesterday, she had never _____ a check.

D. Use a key word in each of these sentences.

    1. The opposite of maximum is _____.

    2. Rubber balls and rubber checks can _____.

    3. She _____her letter in the mail box.

    4. The International Monetary_____(IMF) gives loans to countries.

    5. I _____ my objection; everything's OK now.

    6. I'm going to _____ on my savings account and buy a car.

    7. The company distributed its _____ statement showing its assets, liabilities, and income.

    8. The President is going to make a _____ which will describe her position.

    9. He's not in the regular army; he's in the _____, which would be used only in an emergency.

    10. He has a _____ pilot's license. His business is flying planes.

    11. Stamp collectors like to _____ stamps with each other.

Talk About It

    1. Would you like to work in a bank?

    2. How do you feel when you enter a bank?

    3. Would you do online banking?

    4. Do you have a bank? Do you like it?

7

Borrowing and Lending

At some time or another someone has said, "I'm **broke**. Can you lend me some money?" On a personal level, a loan may only involve two friends who borrow from and lend to each other to help each other. The person who borrows the money **owes** money to the lender. Occasionally the borrower may sign a very simple agreement called an I. O. U. (I owe you). The borrower **repays** the loan when they can, and usually between friends there is no interest charge.

There are times, however, when people need to borrow a large **sum** of money. For example, buying a car requires a large amount of money, and for that we need an auto loan. The interest rate on these kinds of loans is usually rather high, and they are usually for a **term** of not more than a few years.

Another major purchase is a house, and in the United States, banks loan money to people for this. This kind of loan is spread over many years (twenty to thirty years is typical), and it is called a **mortgage**. The bank holds the **deed**, the legal document that proves ownership, until the mortgage is paid off. The home serves as **collateral**: If the borrower fails to repay the loan, the bank repossesses the house. A family celebration called "burning the mortgage" takes place when all the money, interest, and **principal** is finally paid off, and the family at last **owns** their own home.

In addition to making loans to individuals, banks also make loans to businesses. From time to time a business needs to borrow money, and thus go into **debt**, to expand the business. If the business seems to be a good **risk**, the bank will extend **credit** to the business, allowing it to borrow up to a certain amount. The bank becomes the creditor, and the business becomes the debtor.

Countries sometimes need to borrow money, and in the world of international finance, commercial banks often make loans to developing countries. The World Bank, an international development bank, provides special support for long-term development projects. In recent years, however, more and more countries have **defaulted** on their loans, and the list of debtor nations gets longer and longer. It is not only the poor who are in debt. In the United States, Americans have consumed large quantities of foreign goods, but they have not sold as many goods to foreigners. The result is that the United States owes a lot of money to other countries.

With so many people in debt, who are the world's creditors?

broke	sum	deed	own	credit
owe	term	collateral	debt	default
repay	mortgage	principal	risk	

Exercises

A. Underline the correct form of the key word.

1. Last year I (owe, owed, owing) the bank a lot of money, but I finally (repaid, repay, repayment) it. Now I'm broke again.

2. "Mr. Jones, the (term, termination, terminal) of your (mortgaged, mortgage) will be twenty years. The (principality, principle, principal) is $80,000 and the interest is 8.5%. Keep up the (pay, payments) and the (deed, deeded, deeds) will be yours and you'll (owe, own, owner) the house."

3. Because they (default, defaulted) on their previous loan, they are not a good (risky, risk). Therefore, we can't extend (credits, credit, credited) to them.

4. She had never been a (debt, debtor) before, but she needed a large (summary, sum, sums) of money, so she took out a loan and used her home for (collateral, collaterals).

B. Use the key words in the following sentences. Use each key word only once.

1. A period of time can be called a _____.
2. To have no money is to be _____.
3. A piece of paper that specifies the owner of a piece of property is a _____.
4. If I borrow money from you, I _____ you money.
5. This house is mine. I _____ it.
6. If I owe money, I am in _____.
7. If I can't pay back my loan, I am in _____.
8. Another word for "pay back" is _____.
9. A strong, solid business is a good _____.
10. If I give you a loan, I extend_____ to you.
11. The original amount of a loan (excluding interest) is the _____. If it is a long-term loan for property, it is a _____. The house is the _____ . In case the buyer cannot repay, the bank will take the house.
12. Another word for "amount" is _____.

C. Use the correct form of the key word in parentheses.

1. (repay) I _____ that loan a year ago.
2. (owe) How much do I _____ you?
3. (deed) My _____ is registered with the registrar of _____.
4. (broke) "I can't go; I'm_____," he said.
5. (debt) Although his income is up, so are his _____.
6. (term) Do you need a long-_____ loan?
7. (mortgage) All of this property is _____ .
8. (own, collateral) The _____ of the house is really the bank, because the house is the _____ for the loan.
9. (sum) The monthly payment will be the_____ of the principal plus the interest.
10. (risk) The two partners _____ a lot of their own capital when they started the business.
11. (credit) When their business failed, their _____ took all the property and the inventory.
12. (default) Because its currency has lost 50% of its value, New Naciona has_____ on its loan from World Bank.

D. Use a key word in each of these sentences.

1. No, I won't lend you any more money. You already _____ me $15, and I'm almost _____ myself. When you've _____ me we can discuss another loan.
2. At last! We've paid off the_____, and the _____ to the house is ours. We _____ our own home.
3. We needed a short-_____ loan, but the bank turned us down.
4. How can I ever repay my_____ to you? You _____ everything you owned to help me.
5. You've asked for a rather large_____ of money, and the maximum amount of _____ we can give you is only $5,000.
6. They have _____ on both the _____ and the interest.

Talk About It

1. "Neither a borrower nor a lender be." Do you agree?
2. Do you and your friends borrow and lend to each other?
3. What do you know about getting a bank loan?
4. What should you know before you get a loan for a car?

8

Plastic Money

"Will this be cash or **charge**?" In many stores today this is the question a **sales** clerk asks a customer as the customer prepares to pay for what they have purchased. The response, "I'll charge it," means that the customer will pay not with currency or with a check but with a charge card, which is sometimes called plastic money. The more common name for the card is, of course, the credit or debit card. Stores and restaurants everywhere usually display signs to show that they **accept** credit cards.

It can be dangerous to lose your credit card or have it **stolen** by a thief. And because it is so easy to charge purchases, some people buy more things than they should. But credit cards also carry a credit **limit**, meaning there is a maximum **amount** a person may charge. Credit limits are determined by the credit card company. The company decides on a credit **rating** for each card carrier. A person can get a high rating if they are a good risk, and the higher the rating, the more a person can charge.

Credit cards have become very valuable for travelers, and in many cases even a necessity. Nowadays, it is almost impossible to **rent** a car without a credit card. There is one well-known advertisement on TV for a credit card which says, "Don't leave home without it."

Many stores offer their own charge accounts, which enable a customer to charge purchases at that store only. Some places allow people to buy things on time, meaning that the customer can make a **down payment** for part of the total **cost**, and then pay the balance later in regular payments or **installments**. This is called an installment plan. Often there is an additional charge for this service, which is called the finance charge.

ATM
Automatic
Teller Machine

Banks issue a plastic card that can be used with automatic teller machines so that the customer can do their banking after hours and on weekends. This kind of card is called an ATM card. Banks also offer a **debit card**. When a customer uses a debit card, the money **transfer** is done electronically, and the money is withdrawn from the customer's bank account immediately. When a customer gives a card for payment, the clerk will often ask, "Debit or credit?"

Nowadays many people do their shopping online, and a credit or debit card is used to make the payment. Widely used alternatives to credit and debit cards are online payment systems such as PayPal. Another type of payment system is linked to a smartphone. The smartphone user downloads an app such as Apple Pay or Google Pay, and they make a payment with their phone, using this system. These systems provide greater security than paying directly with a card, since the seller does not receive credit card information. Maybe some time in the future paper money will no longer be used for buying and selling?

Exercises

A. Underline the correct form of the key word in parentheses.

1. It's gone! Somebody (steal, stole, stolen) my car.
2. I'd like to open a (charge, charged, charging) account.
3. Will you (accept, accepted, accepting) my Amerbank credit card?
4. In order to increase our (sale, sales), we are having a big end-of-the-year sale. We hope to sell almost everything.
5. He's so rich his credit is (limit, limited, unlimited).
6. How much does this cell phone (cost, costs, costing)?
7. Last year she (rent, rented, renting) an apartment near the university.
8. All of my charges last month (amount, amounted, amounting) to only $85.00. I used my (debiting, debt, debit) card for most things.
9. We closed our savings account and (transfer, transferred, transferring) all our funds to a special account.
10. If you don't pay your bills, you won't get a good credit (rate, rating).

B. Use the key words in the following sentences. Use each key word only once.

1. They_____ all major credit cards at that hotel.
2. You'll need a credit card if you're going to_____ a car.
3. I want to _____ $500 from my checking account to my savings account.
4. The total _____ of this refrigerator is $700. But if you make a _____ _____ of $100, your monthly _____ will be only $50, plus a small finance charge.
5. I can't find my purse. I think it was_____. Fortunately, I was carrying only a small_____ of cash.
6. I don't understand why you won't let me_____ this purchase. My credit_____ is excellent, and on my credit card I have a_____ of $1,000.
7. It has not been a good month. Our _____ have been down by 50%.
8. I prefer to use my _____, because my credit card company charges a fee if I don't pay on time.

C. Use the correct form of the key word in parentheses.

1. (rent) How much is the_____ on this apartment?
2. (accept, debit) We are pleased to announce that we are now _____ all major credit and _____ cards.
3. (installment) She has paid only three _____.
4. (transfer) I have_____ all my money to another account.
5. (cost) The_____ of consumer goods is increasing.
6. (steal) Somebody has been in our room, but I don't think anything was

    _____.

7. (charge) Let's _____ it, instead of paying cash.
8. (Sale) There is a "For _____ " sign on their house.
9. (limit) There is no _____ to the number of transactions you can make on this account.
10. (amount) They stole a huge _____ of money.
11. (payment) The monthly _____ are only $35.

D. Use a key word in each of these sentences.

1. I'm going to_____ to another university.
2. They put all their savings into a _____ on a house.
3. Please_____ my apology.
4. His business lost a rather large _____ of money last year.
5. There is a _____ to the amount we can spend for rent.
6. The_____ clerk forgot to give me my change.
7. When the police finally caught them, they had sold all the _____ works of art.
8. I don't have enough cash; I'll _____ it. I'll put it on my _____ card.
9. He is_____ a room at the hotel that _____ $195 a night. The hotel has a five-star _____.
10. On our new _____ plan, all you need is $10 down.

Talk About It

1. Are credit cards a good thing?
2. What are the dangers of having credit cards?
3. Is it a good idea to let young people have credit cards?
4. Which do you prefer, a credit card or a debit card?

9
Investing

Investing money means saving money so that the value of the money invested will increase, and the money will produce income or profit.

Savings accounts and time deposits (withdrawals are possible only after a specified period of time) are well-known ways of investing money. Another way of investing is to buy **securities**. Stocks and bonds are two kinds of securities that people invest in. A stock, in other terms, means a **share** in some business; so people who buy stocks actually become owners of part of the business – shareholders.

There are two kinds of stocks: common and preferred, and a basic difference between them is that a preferred stock is a **safer** investment, but it is more **expensive** than the lower-**priced** (**cheaper**) common stock.

Why do people invest in stocks? One reason is that stock in a successful company can pay **dividends** (a share of the profit) that are higher than the interest on a savings account. If the company is successful, the value of the share can also increase and the owner of the share can sell it for a high price, and thereby make a profit, which is called a capital **gain**. Of course, the stock market can be risky because some businesses may not do well, and the investor may lose money. In a way, investing in stocks can be like gambling, and for that reason many people rely on a **broker** to advise them and manage their investments by buying and selling securities for them.

Probably the most famous stock exchange is Wall Street in New York City, where millions of shares are traded every day. People with investments follow the stock market reports closely to watch how their stocks are going. When the general **trend** of the market is up, the market is described as "bullish," and when it is down, it is "bearish."

Another form of investment is bonds. A bond is **issued** by a government or a company to raise money. A bond is essentially a loan, and a bondholder does not become an owner of the company, like a shareholder. Although the **yield** on bonds is generally lower than that on good stocks, bonds are usually considered safer.

There are many other ways to invest money. Land and buildings (**real estate**) can be a good investment. Collectibles, such as rare and valuable coins and stamps or works of art are sometimes good investments. In the United States one unusual kind of collectible is the baseball card – small pictures of baseball players that children buy. A 1952 card of the famous baseball player, Mickey Mantle, is worth over $28,500. Purchased for about one cent ($0.01), that is an increase of 2,850,000 percent – a pretty good yield.

Key words

securities	expensive	dividend	trend	real estate
shares	price	gain	issue	
safe	cheap	broker	yield	

Exercises

A. Underline the correct form of the key word.

1. Our company did not pay a (dividend, dividends) this year.
2. In today's trading there were more losers than (gains, gainers, gained).
3. A (broke, broker) must carefully study the (trending, trend, trended) of the market.
4. If the (prices, priced, price) is right, I'll buy.
5. A "blue chip" stock is usually one of the most (expensiver, expensive, expense) ones.
6. Wholesale prices are (more cheap, cheapest, cheaper) than retail prices.
7. Last year they (issue, issues, issued) several thousand new stocks. They were a good investment; they (yield, yielded, yielding) almost $50 a share in dividends.
8. A deed for a house can be given as (security, securities, secure) for a loan.
9. (Real estater, Real estates, Real estate) agents help people buy and sell houses and land.
10. These (share, sharing, shares) are a (safest, safe, safety) investment.

B. Use one of the key words in the sentences below. Use each key word only once.

1. This computer is very_____, but the more _____ one is a better buy because it can do more.
2. I bought that stock when the _____ was $47.00 and sold it recently for $87.00. My _____ was $40.00.
3. Stocks and bonds are _____. Another word for secure is _____.
4. I'm going to call my_____ and have her sell all my _____ in that company.
5. This bond will _____ 5%.
6. She received a very nice _____ this year from her ABM stock.
7. This is a listing of all the new bond _____.
8. She owns a lot of valuable _____ on the Pacific Coast.
9. Recently, the market _____ has been bullish.

C. Use the correct form of the key word in parentheses.

1. (expensive, cheap) We have three kinds. This one is the most _____ ; this one is medium-priced, and this one is the _____.
2. (price) He bought the highest- _____ model.
3. (security) I think the best _____ you can buy is this one.
4. (share) She owns a hundred _____ of Macrosoft stock.
5. (safe) I think a savings account is the _____ kind of investment.
6. (broker) _____ are agents who work for a brokerage firm.
7. (gain) My USTEL stock _____ three points yesterday.
8. (trend) I think you'll see a new _____ in the market.
9. (issue) Do you think they will ever re-_____ the Susan B. Anthony one-dollar coin?
10. (dividend) _____ can be expressed in dollars or in percentage.
11. (yield) The current _____ on our CD (certificate of deposit) is 3.5%.
12. (real estate) I don't own any _____ or securities.

D. Use the correct form of one of the key words in each of these sentences.

1. A large box that can be locked and is used for storing valuable things is a _____.
2. My_____ is D.P. Dutton.
3. Did your stock _____ or lose today?
4. Although she drives a very _____ car, her clothes are obviously used and _____.
5. What a_____ to pay! One simple mistake cost her a fortune.
6. The _____ in car-buying is toward the smaller, hybrid models and away from SUVs. However, the _____ market is doing well with larger homes.
7. The Post Office has _____ a new express mail stamp.
8. Your year-end _____ check is in the mail.
9. The principal _____ holder owns 42% of the shares.
10. SEC stands for _____ and Exchange Commission, a U.S. government agency.
11. Another word for _____ is "give."

Talk About It

1. If you had a sum of money to invest, what would you invest in?
2. What is a bad investment nowadays?
3. Would you use a broker or do your own investing?
4. Would you consider being a broker or a real estate investor?

10

Budgeting and Accounting

Everyone would agree that it is easy to spend money - sometimes too easy - and it is difficult to save money. And who has not said, after **counting** the money in their purse, "Where did my money go?" So before and after earning, spending, and saving, people and businesses turn to paper, pencil, and computers to plan what is going to happen with their money and to **account** for what is happening or has happened to it.

A financial plan is called a budget, and our language has many phrases related to our budgets - staying within the budget, living within one's means, over-spending, cost overruns, and budget deficits, for example.

This universal problem affects not only the individual, but all **entities** – small businesses, big corporations, nonprofit organizations, and of course, governments. Many politicians have made many speeches about cost overruns and budget **deficits** caused by expenses being greater than income. Husbands and wives worry about living within their means, and parents caution children about over-spending their **allowances**.

A budget is, quite simply, a **forecast** of what the **revenue** will be (how much money will come in) and what the **expenses** will be (how much money will go out). Some expenses are the result of purchases, and accountants call these purchases expenditures. If the budget is for a profit-making entity, the revenue should exceed the expenses and the **bottom line** should show a profit. The family hopes to have a balanced budget, and politicians often demand that the government balance its budget, too.

Budgets are prepared for certain periods of time. For example, a one-year accounting period is called a **fiscal** year. When the year begins, it then becomes the task of the bookkeeper to record or enter the income and expenses in journals and ledgers. The accountant then, in a sense, counts up and analyzes the financial status and the financial progress of the entity. The financial status is shown in a balance sheet, which shows the **assets** (what is owned), the **liabilities** (what is owed), and the **equities** (how much capital the business has). The accountant prepares a financial statement, which has – in addition to the balance sheet – the income statement, which shows the important bottom line and the entity's profit or loss.

Key words

count	deficit	revenue	fiscal	equity
account	allowance	expense	asset	
entities	forecast	bottom line	liability	

Exercises

A. Underline the correct form of the key word.

1. If there is a (deficits, deficit), it may be because the (revenues, revenue) are not enough.
2. The (fiscally, fiscal) year may not be the same as the calendar year.
3. We get a daily (allow, allowing, allowance) for food and lodging when we are traveling.
4. A person who makes a forecast is a (forecastist, forecaster).
5. I need to approve all (expensive, expenses).
6. The (accounter, accountant, accountist) has set up a new system of (accountable, accounts).
7. (Asset, Assets) minus (liabilities, liables) equal (equity, equality).
8. Yesterday I (count, countered, counted) all our cash.
9. An (entity, entities) is something that exists; therefore a (non-entity, un-entity) doesn't exist.
10. The (bottom lines, bottom line) is that we didn't have a profit.

B. Use the key words in the following sentences. Use each word only once.

1. If money is spent, it is an _____.
2. Money that is earned is _____.
3. If expenses are greater than revenues, there is a _____.
4. Money that is owed is a _____.
5. Money that is owned is an _____ .
6. Assets minus liabilities equal _____, or capital.
7. A balanced budget shows a _____ _____ that does not have a deficit.
8. Let's _____ our money and see how much we have.
9. Corporations are _____.
10. He gives his children an _____ of $20.00 each per week.
11. The government's_____ year begins on July 1.
12. A look into the future can be called a _____.
13. "You've got to_____ for every dollar you've spent," said his angry wife.

C. Use the correct form of the key word in parentheses.

1. (deficit) The United States has a trade _____ with China.
2. (liability) Our assets are greater than our _____.
3. (allow) We are not _____ to spend any money in that account.
4. (account) There's something wrong here, and I can't _____ for it.
5. (count) Her son was in his room, _____ all his money.
6. (revenue) For the government, taxes are _____.
7. (fiscal) To be in good financial health is to be _____ healthy.
8. (Forecast) _____ the weather will never be an exact science.
9. (expense) The military accounts for 40% of the government's _____.
10. (entity) Several of his _____ had a profit this year.
11. (asset, equity, bottom line) Our increase in _____ resulted in an increase in our _____, so the _____ _____) looks very good.

D. Use a key word in each of these sentences.

1. The_____ for tomorrow is for more rain.
2. The_____ for meals is $40 a day.
3. The_____ _____ is this: We lost money last year.
4. To be "in the black" is to show a profit. To be "in the red" is to have a _____.
5. The government agency responsible for collecting taxes is the Internal _____ Service.
6. "This administration is _____ irresponsible. Vote for me and for_____ responsibility."
7. Cash, equipment, and buildings are _____.
8. After we pay our _____, the balance is the owners' _____.
9. Don't _____ your chickens before they hatch.
10. "You're nothing!" he shouted, "You're a non-_____!"
11. We've got to reduce our _____ this month, or we'll be in the red again.
12. "What _____ should I charge this expense to?" asked the bookkeeper.

Talk About It

1. Do you keep good financial records?
2. Do you have someone help you with tax returns?
3. Would you consider being an accountant?
4. Do you have a personal budget?

11
Insurance

The purpose of insurance is to provide financial **compensation** to people and organizations when something unexpected or **disastrous** happens and the result is financial loss. In a way, insurance companies offer **protection** so that an accident, a severe health problem, a fire, or a natural disaster, such as a flood, will not result in a financial disaster to a family or business entity.

The first form of insurance **coverage** was marine insurance, provided by Lloyd's of London in 1689 to protect shipowners and merchants from loss if a ship sank with its cargo. Nowadays many different kinds of policies are offered.

Policyholders commonly insure their health, their property (especially homes and autos), and their lives, and they also carry liability protection. Liability insurance protects the policyholder against a legal suit in which somebody may **sue** the policyholder, claiming that the policyholder was responsible for damage that the plaintiff (the person who sues) suffered.

For families, it is important of course, to protect their major investments, and so they insure their homes against fire and the family car against damage from accidents. In recent years, automobile insurance, especially liability protection, has become very expensive, and in many places it is **compulsory**, which means the family members cannot use the car if they do not have insurance. For some families in the United States, especially those with teenage drivers, the **premiums** may be well over $1,000 a year.

Health insurance is also very important to the family, because the cost of health care has become very high. One way in which the cost of the premiums can be reduced is to carry a high **deductible** amount. This means that the family would pay for the first $500, for example, of the costs, and the insurance company would then pay for the rest, after the first $500 has been deducted. A form of health insurance called **disability** insurance is also carried by many working people. If they are disabled and cannot work – perhaps because of a broken arm - they will receive money from the insurance company.

Life insurance is paid when a person dies. The **beneficiaries** of the policy will receive money to cover the lost wages that the dead person can no longer earn. This kind of protection is especially important for families with small children, where it may be difficult for the surviving parent to work and care for the children.

Another kind of insurance provides the financial security a person needs when they retire and no longer earn wages or a salary. Most people, while they are working, belong to a retirement plan, and then when they retire, they receive a **pension**. In the United States there is a compulsory retirement and health insurance plan called Social Security and Medicare. For many older people the arrival of their monthly pension check is a very important event, even though it is barely enough to meet everyday expenses.

Key words

compensation	coverage	compulsory	disability
disaster	policy	premium	beneficiary
protection	sue	deductible	pension

Exercises

A. Underline the correct form of the key word.

1. A person who receives a pension can be called a (pensioner, pension).
2. A person who receives benefits is a (beneficient, beneficiary).
3. A person who receives disability payments is (disabling, disabled).
4. A deductible amount is a (deducter, deduction).
5. The person who owns the policy is the (policeman, policyholder, politician).
6. A person who has insurance coverage is (covering, covered).
7. A person who has protection is (protector, protected).
8. A person who receives compensation is (compensating, compensated).
9. A person who (sue, sues, sueing) files a legal suit.
10. The results of a disaster are (disasterous, disastrous).
11. In some countries, participation in national insurance is (compulsive, compulsory).
12. Installment payments are sometimes called (premium, premiums).

B. Use the key words above in the following sentences. Use each key word only once.

1. She's retired now and living on her _____.
2. In this state you must have liability insurance; it's _____.
3. A good insurance_____ will give your family _____ against financial disaster.
4. What a_____ ! Everything was destroyed.
5. He can't work now because of his illness, but he has_____ insurance, so he is receiving some money.
6. His wife was the _____ of his life insurance policy.
7. The _____for this policy is only $15 a month, and for that you get _____of $10,000.
8. He threatened to take them to court and _____ them for a million dollars.
9. This policy carries a $200 _____ amount. After you pay $200, the company will pay the rest.
10. "This check is little _____ for the loss of your husband, Mrs. Johnson, but I'm sure he would be happy to know that you won't have any financial worries."

C. Use the correct form of the key word in parentheses.

1. (policy) He owns several _____.
2. (beneficiary) She listed her children as _____.
3. (cover) This policy will give you complete _____. The (premium) _____ are only $250 a month.
4. (compensate) You will be_____ for your work.
5. (protect) Your family will be fully_____ if you should die. They will also receive money from your _____(pension, pensioner).
6. (disable) He is a_____ veteran of the Vietnam War.
7. (deduct) After_____ your expenses from your allowance, you should write the balance due here.
8. (disaster) The stock market crash of 1987 was _____.
9. (sue) This liability coverage will protect you in case you are _____.
10. (compulsory) I don't have to do that; it's not _____.

D. Use one of the key words in each of these sentences.

1. My automobile insurance _____ cost me about $800 last year.
2. The sinking of the *Titanic,* with the loss of hundreds of lives, was one of the worst _____ of the twentieth century.
3. "Don't worry, I'll_____ you," said the little boy to his frightened sister.
4. As the _____ of her life insurance policy, he received $50,000 when she died.
5. The _____ should be paid by the end of the month.
6. "I'll_____ you for that!" shouted the angry man.
7. All the employees have to pay into the company's _____ fund. Each month the company _____ 10% from its employees' paychecks. It is a _____ deduction. The employees can retire at age 65.
8. He has been_____ and unable to work for the last five years.
9. I expected to be _____ for my services. I didn't think I was working for nothing.
10. All the TV networks will cover the election tonight. The _____ will begin at 6 p.m. and go all night long.

Talk About It

1. What kind of insurance should people have? What kind is not so important?
2. Should the government offer health insurance for all?
3. Have you ever collected any compensation from an insurance company? Was it easy?

12
Gambling

One of the most common verbs in the English language is "**bet**." English speakers frequently use it simply to mean "think" or "believe," and in some areas of the United States "you bet" means "okay" or "yes." But for the gambler, the word "bet" is almost always followed by phrases such as "two dollars." The gambler's bet is a **wager**, and his goal is to **win** the wager and make money, just as a laborer earns wages or a businessman makes a profit. However, gambling is a risky way to earn a living, and in many places gambling is not permitted; it is **illegal**.

There are many ways to gamble, and almost everyone has gambled in one way or another. Probably the most common form of gambling is the lottery, in which large numbers of people buy tickets with a number on them, hoping to get the **lucky** number and win a **huge** sum of money, becoming instant millionaires. Winning at the lottery is purely a matter of luck.

People also like to bet on sporting events, where, in addition to luck, a little knowledge may be helpful. For most people this is done with friends who make a wager on the outcome of a football game, for example. One sport in particular, horse racing, has become more of a gambling event than a sporting event.

Much of the vocabulary of gambling has developed from horse racing. In horse racing, there is a system based on the past performance of the horses. A horse that has done well in the past and is expected to win the race is the **favorite**. People who accept bets (bookmakers or bookies) give **odds** on the horse's chance of winning. It is not so risky to bet on the favorite, and so a person who places a bet on the favorite would not win as much money as the person who makes a bet on a horse that has not done so well in the past. Betting on a horse with a poor or unknown record is sometimes called "taking a long shot," and the horse itself is sometimes called a "dark horse."

Many games have also become associated with gambling. One that is especially well known is the card game called poker. As in horse racing, a lot of words used in poker have become popular idioms. Two of the most common ones are "**pass**," when a player does not want to bet, and "**fold**," when a player does not want to continue the game, perhaps because the **stakes** are too high, meaning that the results for winners and losers will be large winnings and large losses.

There are many other games of **chance**, from simple games like Bingo to the more complicated ones that use dice or machines such as roulette wheels and slot machines - also known as "one-armed bandits."

Regardless of the kind of gambling, it is Lady Luck who, more often than not, gives and takes pennies and **fortunes**.

bet	won	huge	pass	chance
wagered	legalizing	favorite	folded	fortune
	unlucky	odds	stakes	

Exercises

A. Underline the correct form of the key word.

1. (Bet, Betting, Bettors) can become an addiction. Some people gamble away all their money.
2. The lottery (won, winner, winnings) gave all his prize money to UNICEF.
3. It is (illegal, illegalized, illegally) in any state for children to gamble.
4. Although it didn't look like rain when I left home this morning, (lucky, luck, luckily) I brought an umbrella.
5. That bear is the (hugest, huge, hugely) animal I have ever seen.
6. I don't understand why you (pass, passed, passing) in the last bridge hand. I thought you had a lot of points and wanted to raise the bid.
7. Companies that cannot keep up with the competition are forced to (fold, folding) or to sell out to larger corporations.
8. The (favorite, favoritism) didn't win the race. It came in third.
9. The (oddity, oddly, odds) are not in his favor.
10. I didn't plan on meeting her; I met her by (chance, chanced).
11. It was (fortune, fortunate, fortunately) that we were able to meet.
12. I am (staked, staking, stakes) my reputation on your winning the race.
13. He is crazy to (wager, wagered, wagering) such a large sum on such a long shot.

B. Use the key words above in the following sentences. Use each word only once.

1. I'll _____ you $10 that the Boston Celtics will beat the Los Angeles Lakers in tonight's game.
2. He made a _____ fortune by investing in computers.
3. You are gambling with your life when you drink and drive, and those _____ are too high for anyone to pay.
4. If you are betting on Number 5, the _____ are 3 to 1.
5. Games of _____ bore me, because there is no skill involved.
6. How many games has the school basketball team_____ so far?
7. When I bet on a horse, I usually select the safer _____, although occasionally I will put my money on a dark horse just for fun.

8. Thanks for the invitation tonight, but I'll have to _____ as I have a lot of work to complete before tomorrow's meeting.

9. The Kennedy family's _____ came from investments in the railroads.

10. Franklin often went to the race track, but he never _____ more than ten dollars.

11. I wasn't surprised that his company _____; it had been overextended in its loans for months.

12. A few states are now _____ gambling to provide added sources of state revenues.

13. This is the thirteenth sentence. Many people think thirteen is an _____ number.

C. Use the correct form of the key word in parentheses.

1. (bet) He _____ and lost all his salary last night at the casino and I'll _____ he will do same thing again next payday.

2. (fold) So far, all of her businesses have _____.

3. (win) You must declare all your lottery _____ to the government.

4. (stake) Because his brother _____ him to $100, Albert was able to enter the game and win.

5. (fortune) That was a very un_____ move you made; I can now win the game.

6. (legal) The use of marijuana has been _____ in several states.

7. (wager) He was drunk when he made that _____.

8. (huge) The university is grateful for her _____contribution.

9. (odds) I'll give _____ of three to one that he doesn't come on time.

10. (favorite) Teachers try not to have _____ students, because _____ is not fair.

11. (luck) Some people carry _____ charms, such as a four-leaf clover, a rabbit's foot, or a new penny, hoping these things will bring good _____.

12. (pass) In the card game of bridge, three _____ automatically require that a new hand be dealt.
13. (chance) What do you think the Democratic candidate's _____ are for winning the election this time?

D. Use each of the key words in these sentences.

1. It is better to quit while you are ahead in this game; the _____ will only get higher and higher.
2. The_____are very high that Prince Charles will replace Queen Elizabeth as Britain's monarch.
3. Would you like to take a _____ on the lottery? The tickets are only five dollars.
4. Since I don't know the answer, I'll _____ on that question.
5. For me there is a _____ difference between fresh-brewed coffee and instant coffee.
6. Every Olympic athlete dreams of _____ a gold medal.
7. Many investors lost a _____ in the autumn stock market crash known as Black Monday.
8. When a business _____, we say it has "gone out of business."
9. He bet on number three and won; his two-dollar _____ paid twenty dollars.
10. Four is usually my _____ number, but tonight I'm losing.
11. It is usually safe to bet on the _____ , as that horse nearly always wins something.
12. He is in the country _____ and is afraid of being deported if found without a passport.
13. To place a _____, gamblers call a bookmaker to _____ on the team, number, horse, or whatever they hope will win money for them.

Talk About It

1. Should gambling be illegal?
2. What kind of gambling have you done?
3. Have you ever won any money?
4. Do you have a lucky number?

13
Changing Money

Changing money can mean two things: changing a large bill or coin into smaller bills or coins, such as changing a five-dollar bill into five ones, or exchanging two currencies, for example, dollars for euros. In the first instance, there are times when a person needs small **change** (we usually think of small change as coins) or when a person has a high-**denomination** banknote and wants to get smaller denominations. In the second instance, changing currencies, we enter into a very complex world of the foreign exchange market.

Just as our world does not have only one language as the medium of communication, neither do we have a single **monetary** system as the medium of international exchange. Any traveler experiences this when they go to another country. One of the first things they must do is find a place to **convert** their money, and one of their first questions will be, "What is the exchange rate?" As we all know, exchange rates can vary from day to day and from place to place.

One place in particular, the black market, often has a rate that is better than the **official** rate.

As our world shrinks and it becomes easier to carry out trade across international boundaries, the **volume** of trade increases, and therefore the **flow** of money increases. Large numbers of businesses become involved in **exporting** and **importing** goods. If a businessperson exports their product to another country, they are going to receive money from a company or person in another country. Businesspeople, therefore, need the services of a money changer, and so they turn to banks. A bank, then, becomes the middleman, arranging for the exchange of money across national boundaries.

In the world of international trade, some currencies are more desirable than others. The currencies of some countries are not very **stable**, and **inflation** may cause the currency to continuously lose its value. In some cases a government may officially devalue its own currency. In other cases the currency may be allowed to **float**, meaning that the value of the currency will go up or down according to the demand for it.

Currencies are traded on the foreign exchange market, which is an international market with major centers in London, Frankfurt, Zurich, Tokyo, Hong Kong, and New York. At these markets traders buy and sell currencies from each other. Many of the traders are from international banks and large corporations, but there are also individual **speculators,** who are trying to make a profit by watching the exchange rates very closely and buying and selling currencies - hoping to buy low and sell high.

```
┌─────────────────────────────────────────────────────────────────┐
│                          Key words                                │
│   change        convert      flow        stable      float        │
│   denomination  official     exports     inflation   speculate     │
│   monetary      volume       imports                              │
└─────────────────────────────────────────────────────────────────┘
```

Exercises

A. Underline the correct form of the key word.

1. I need some coins. Do you have any (changes, change)?
2. Last year the U.S. (exported, export) less than it (imported, import).
3. With this conversion table, you can easily (convert, convertible) dollars and other currencies.
4. There has been a constant (float, flow, flowed) of dollars to other countries.
5. The new policy has not been (official, officially) announced.
6. Financial (stable, stability) is not easy to achieve.
7. I think the new policy is (inflation, inflationary).
8. (Speculator, Speculation) means taking a risk, hoping to make a large profit.
9. When a currency is (floating, flotation), its value rises and falls with supply and demand.
10. The Central Bank establishes (monetarily, monetary) policies.

B. Use the key words above in the following sentences. Use each word only once.

1. Goods that go out of the country are _____ , and goods that come in are _____ .
2. The _____ exchange rate is 3.5 to 1, but on the black market you can get 3.8.
3. The IMF is the International _____ Fund. It loans money for development.
4. Excuse me, sir. Can you _____ a 10,000-yen note?
5. The government is concerned about the _____ of capital out of the country.
6. The _____ of imports has increased again this year.
7. I'd like to_____ pounds to yuan.
8. What is the highest _____ of the euro?
9. _____ is reducing the purchasing power of our earnings.
10. The government has decided to_____ the lira rather than devalue it.
11. The stock market seems to be _____ again after a series of ups and downs.
12. He thought the Mexican peso would go up, so he decided to _____ and buy several million.

C. Use the correct form of the key words in these sentences.

1. (import, export) He imports goods. He's an _____.
   She exports goods. She's an _____.
2. (convert) Last week I _____ all my lira to rubles.
3. (change) I need some coins. Do you have any _____?
4. (denomination) He had bills of every_____in his wallet.
5. (official) This will only be_____when it is
   _____approved by a government _____.
6. (stable) The president said that we had achieved economic _____.
7. (monetary) Several years ago the British modified their _____
   system so that there are now 100 pence to the pound rather than 240.
8. (Inflation) _____ increases when demand exceeds supply.
9. (float) Just as currency can be _____, an exchange rate can be called a
   _____exchange rate.
10. (Speculate)_____ are buying South African rands.
11. (flow, volume) There has been a constant _____ of dollars out of the country,
    and the_____ of imports has not decreased at all.

D. Use a key word in each of these sentences.

1. I don't have any _____. Can you lend me a few coins?
2. First he _____euros to pounds, and then he sold his pounds for
   yen. His_____ brought him a profit of over twenty thousand
   dollars. Not bad, for a day's work.
3. Hyundais are _____ by the Koreans to the U.S., and the
   U.S. _____ Saabs from Sweden.
4. When Lee first arrived in Turkey the _____ rate was over 10,000 lira to
   the dollar. A few years later, the new lira was about 1.34 to the dollar.
5. The prices of new cars have gone up by 30%, while the overall _____
   rate is only 10%.
6. The hero did not expect a _____ reward. Nevertheless, he was
   pleased to receive the $5,000.
7. She asked for $1,000 in small _____ – tens and twenties only.
8. The patient's condition has been _____ now, so we expect she will recover.
9. The empty boat was found_____on the water.
10. To increase or decrease the amount of sound on the radio, turn the _____ knob.
11. The amount of water _____ through the dam has decreased in the past few days.

Tourists exchanging money in Pattaya City, Thailand, a resort city.

Talk About It

1. Do you know the value of some other currencies based on the U.S. Dollar?
2. How many currencies have you ever used?
3. Should the Americas all use the dollar, like the Euro in Europe?
4. Would you like to be a currency trader?

14
Money and Crime

"Money is the root of all evil" is an old saying. Obviously, it is not true, but many crimes are **committed** to get money. There are many kinds of financial crimes; some of them are a form of stealing – taking money illegally. **Cheating** is another kind of crime that can involve money. A cheater gets money by tricks or dishonest means such as charging too much for something.

One of the oldest kinds of stealing is armed **robbery**. One person, a robber, with a weapon forces another person to give up their money. In older times, travelers were stopped and robbed on the road. This was known as highway robbery – a term that is still used today to mean the price or cost of something is too high. Sometimes **thieves** don't steal just money. Their theft may be an automobile or other valuable things which they sell for money or keep for personal use. Nowadays many robberies are committed by people with serious drug addiction problems.

At sea, robbers are called **pirates**. Years ago they robbed **merchant** ships, looking for gold, silver, and other valuable things. Even today, pirates sometimes attack boats at sea. Nowadays another kind of pirate copies books, music CDs, DVDs, and computer games and programs. An individual may think this is a very small thing, and that "everybody does it," but it is stealing, and when millions of people do it, this kind of piracy cheats writers, performers, and the entertainment and computer industries.

Some financial crimes are not so obvious. A worker may secretly steal money from a company and use it for themselves. This crime is known as **embezzlement**. This person is guilty of **fraud** – unfair or unlawful gain. **Corruption** is another form of stealing. Often it refers to a government officer cheating the government by taking money for themselves from government accounts.

Individuals may also try to cheat the government by not paying their taxes. People guilty of this crime are tax **evaders**. When the Internal Revenue Service thinks an entity, either a person or a business, may be paying too little tax, it may **audit** the entity's books. If the evader is caught, they may pay a large **penalty**. Some crimes at the highest level of the economy involve the officers of a huge corporation. They may do a variety of things to show the government and the public that their corporation is financially healthy, when in fact it is not. The result is that investors can lose a lot of money when this "white-collar crime" is discovered, and the corporation's stocks lose most of their value. Crimes at this level can have a big effect on the entire economy. The corporate officers may have to pay a very large **fine**, and they may be sent to jail.

There are two other kinds of crimes; one old, and the other new. Counterfeiting, printing fake money, has existed for centuries. **Money laundering** has become a serious illegal activity. "Dirty" money (money obtained by illegal means) is used in a variety of financial transactions and emerges as "clean" money. It's an important way for criminals and terrorists to hide the source of their money and make it useable.

Key words

committed	thieves	embezzle	evasion	fine
cheat	pirate	fraud	audited	money laundering
robbed	merchant	corruption	penalized	

Exercises

A. Underline the correct form of the key word in the parentheses.

1. The (merchants, merchandise) in this city are doing well.
2. (Pirates, Piracy, Pirate) is a form of robbery.
3. It is a crime to (evade, evasion, evasive) paying taxes.
4. The drunk driver was (fine, fines, fined) $500.00.
5. The (thief, theft, thieves) were caught with the stolen goods.
6. The (robber, robbery, rob) was (committed, commit, committee) at 9:00.
7. "You're a (fraud, fraudulent)," she cried. "You're (cheater, cheating, cheat) me, you thief!"
8. The bookkeeper (embezzlement, embezzled, embezzling) thousands of dollars last year.
9. The FBI suspects that Offcoast Bank is a (money laundering, money launderer).
10. (Corrupted, Corrupts, Corruption) hurts the economy.
11. In this state, the (penal, penalty, penalize) for speeding is a large fine.

B. Use one of the key words above in the following sentences. Use each word only once.

1. A _____ buys and sells things.
2. The _____ Blackbeard robbed and sank many ships.
3. The government _____ the Steelwell Company and discovered five years of tax _____. The _____ was a _____ of 450,000 dollars.
4. Terrorists turn drug money into clean money by _____ it.
5. A gang _____ the State Street Bank, and escaped. The _____ got away with half a million dollars.
6. They have _____ robberies in several states.
7. "This man is a _____. He is trying to _____ us."
8. The company's accountant tried to _____ thousands of dollars from the pension plan.
9. The World Bank is trying to stop _____ in Lower Robovia.

C. Use the correct form of each key word in parentheses.

1. (merchant) A _____ buys and sells _____.
2. (pirate) Once upon a time _____ sailed from this port.
3. (evade) Tax _____ is a serious mistake.
4. (fine) He was _____ five thousand dollars by the judge.
5. (thief) Several _____ broke into the house and stole everything.
6. (commit) Butch Cassidy _____ many robberies.
7. (embezzle) She _____ a lot of money from her company and then escaped to Mexico.
8. (money laundering) "I am not a _____ _____, " he said.
9. (corruption) There are too many _____ officials in this country.
10. (fraud) Beware of _____ when a caller says you have won the lottery.
11. (cheat) You have four aces and I have one. I think you're _____ us.
12. (audit) Last week our _____ checked our tax return and found it to be OK.
13. (penalty) If you don't report all your income, you may be hit with a stiff _____.
14. (rob) Robin Hood _____ the rich and gave to the poor.

D. Use a key word in each of these sentences.

1. Another word for goods is _____.
2. In some parts of the world, _____ still stop and _____ ships.
3. The speeding driver _____ the road block.
4. Thieves can use _____ to make their illegal money clean.
5. Another word for "make" or "do" is "_____."
6. The treasurer _____ thousands before she was caught.
7. Her husband has a love in another state; he is _____ on her.
8. A virus _____ the company's computers.
9. The _____ revealed that the company was missing thousands.
10. A person who is a _____ usually tries to cheat you.
11. The _____ can be a _____ or even several days in jail.
12. The thief broke into the store and opened the safe. The _____ was over ten thousand dollars.

Talk About It

1. Have you ever been cheated or robbed? How did you feel?
2. What's the worst kind of financial crime?
3. Is copying a DVD really a big problem?
4. Would you ever evade paying some taxes?

15
Money and the Internet

It's easy to forget that not long ago, nobody had a computer, and the internet really didn't exist as it does today. The computer has made the internet possible, and this new technology has changed the way people use money. Nowadays it is almost possible for people to carry only "plastic money" in their **wallets**.

Many financial transactions can now be done for us by electronic transfer from one computer to another. A salary check and other forms of income can be deposited directly into a checking account, and bills can be paid automatically on a regular basis. There is no need to write a check, find an envelope and stamp, and take it to the post office.

With a personal computer, a telephone, a credit or debit card, and a bank account, people can now **manage** their money without leaving home. In fact, smart phone users need only their phones to purchase, pay for, even sell things, and get on planes.
Debit cards are linked to a checking account, and the money is withdrawn from the checking account immediately. Unlike the credit card, the debit card user usually has to enter a PIN (personal identification number). Eventually, even checks could become

obsolete, no longer used, as debit cards (also called check cards) become more popular.

Shopping and making purchases are now done **online** with a computer. The consumer goes to the internet and finds a **website** that offers a product they want. They click on "buy" or "add to my shopping cart," and then they give their credit or debit card information: the card number, the **expiration** date, and card security **code** number on the back of the card. The purchase is delivered a few days later. Retail stores on Main Street USA are, in fact, losing money to internet sales.

The internet has also contributed a new way to **advertise** products. A consumer can **subscribe** to a company's newsletter or information service and receive regular offers from the company. One form of internet advertising has become a problem for users of electronic mail (email). Every day, millions of unwanted messages called **spam** are sent to email users with offers for insurance, mortgages, health products, investment opportunities, and many other things.

There is also a danger with email accounts. Some email offers are simply frauds. They make promises they cannot deliver, and the consumer is cheated. In some cases, fraudulent spammers ask for personal information such as a credit card or social security number, and they use this information to get money from the person's accounts or use the person's credit card illegally. This activity is called a **scam**, and many people have lost a lot of money to the scammers. This crime is called **ID theft** (ID = identity). In fact, ID theft can be done in a variety of ways, and can be a very **lucrative** crime. The thief gains a lot of money or goods quickly and easily, and consumers lose millions of dollars to ID theft. The computer age has changed the ways we use money and changed the ways thieves steal money.

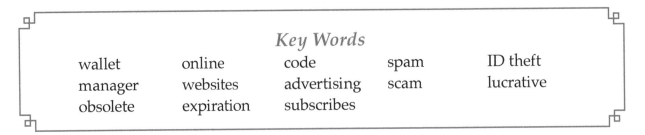

Key Words

wallet	online	code	spam	ID theft
manager	websites	advertising	scam	lucrative
obsolete	expiration	subscribes		

Exercises

A. Underline the correct form of the key word in the parentheses.

1. He lost his (wallets, wallet) with all his cash and credit cards.
2. A person who is searching the internet is (online, onlining, onlined).
3. A (scam, scammed) is a kind of fraud.
4. You can (manager, manage, managing) your account online.
5. Many people have lost money to (ID thefting, ID thieves).
6. Our company spends a huge amount of money on (advertise, advertisements).
7. Unwanted email advertising is called (spam, scam).
8. A (subscription, subscribe, subscriber) pays money to receive newsletters.
9. Some people think that the internet will make newspapers (obsolete, obsolescence).
10. He sold his business for millions. It was obviously a very (lucrative, luxury) business.
11. "I saw that book on your (website, internet, online)."
12. Somehow he got my card number, the (expiry, expiration, expire) date, and the security (coding, code, encode).

B. Use the key words above in the following sentences. Use each word only once.

1. She buys a lot of her clothes _____.
2. I complained to the _____ of the bank.
3. My friend manages several _____.
4. This morning my email account was filled with _____. I put it in my junk box.
5. Our family _____ to several magazines.
6. We paid a lot for that _____. I hope it sells a lot of our product.
7. "Do you think the one-cent coin will become _____?"
8. _____ is a serious crime.
9. A robber stole my _____.
10. The _____ date is 03/29.
11. My three-digit security _____ is 306.
12. It was a very _____ _____. They stole thousands of dollars.

C. Use the correct form of the key word in parentheses.

1. (subscribe, expire) My _____ to Lifetime Magazine will
   _____ next month.
2. (online, website) She went _____ and checked out their _____.
3. (spam, scam) The email seemed to be important, but it was just _____. She
   responded but it was also a _____ and the scammer emptied her bank account.
4. (lucrative). ID theft must be a very _____ crime.
5. (code, ID theft). The card's security _____ helps prevent _____.
6. (advertise, manage) She is the _____ _____ for
   Hopewell Products, Inc.
7. (wallet) I always buy leather _____.
8. (obsolete) Typewriters are _____

D. Use a key word in each of these sentences.

1. You can _____ your account _____ with your computer.
2. Is managing a _____ a very _____ job?
3. If an emailer asks for your bank account information, it may be a _____.
   Don't give it out.
4. I _____ to an online newsletter.
5. Your card has an _____ date on the front and a security _____
   number on the back.
6. She gave him her card number and she was the victim of _____.
7. Throwing away _____ email messages takes a lot of time. This form of
   _____ should be controlled.
8. The Air Museum displays many _____ aircraft.

Talk About It

1. What kind of financial transactions do you do on the internet?
2. Do you prefer to shop online or in person at a store?
3. What can be done about spam?
4. What can we do to prevent ID theft?

16
Death and Taxes

It is sometimes said that the only sure things in life are death and taxes. Death is, of course, a certainty. Taxation exists wherever there is a government, and since virtually everyone lives under the government of one of the world's 170 nations, taxes are a certainty.

There are many kinds of taxes, but the two that are found almost everywhere are sales taxes and income taxes. Sales tax is paid when we buy something. It is usually **calculated** as a **percentage** (for example, 5 percent) of the price of the thing purchased. Income tax, which is also called **withholding** tax, is a tax people pay on their earnings.

Although there are many ways in which income taxes are collected, the system that is used in the United States is typical. A wage-earner's tax is based on a percentage of his earnings, and that percentage increases as the earnings increase. Employees are allowed a certain number of **exemptions**, which reduce their taxable income. Exemptions are given for the number of dependents (children and other non-working family members) that the worker supports. Tax tables are often used to calculate the amount that the employer should withhold from the employee's paycheck. Self-employed people or people with irregular incomes must **estimate** the amount of tax they will owe and pay it in installments.

April 15 is a well-known date in the United States. It is the deadline for **filing** tax returns with the Internal Revenue Service. Every person must report their **gross** income, which is the total amount they earned; claim their deductions for exemptions and other deductible expenses; and then pay tax on their **net** taxable income. In simple terms, net equals gross minus deductions. In some cases, people choose to **itemize** their deductions if they have a lot of deductible expenses. They list, item by item, all the deductible expenses they have had during the year. Medical expenses, for example, are deductible. Everyone hopes that after all the **computations** they will find they have paid too much in taxes, and the government will give them a **refund**.

The other certainty, death, brings an end to concerns about taxes, but the person who dies usually leaves some wealth behind for others to be concerned about. What is left – money and property – is called the estate, and directions for who shall **inherit** the estate are contained in the **will**. Many a novel and murder mystery has been written about the death and will of a rich old man whose final words are: "And to my personal secretary, Miss Muggeridge, I leave my entire fortune."

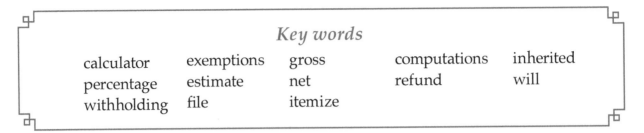

Key words

calculator	exemptions	gross	computations	inherited
percentage	estimate	net	refund	will
withholding	file	itemize		

Exercises

A. Underline the correct form of the key word in parentheses.

1. How much was (withheld, withholding) from your paycheck last month?
2. Computations are done by a (compute, computer) and a calculator
   does (calculates, calculations).
3. Inflation has increased by 8 (percentage, percent).
4. The officer (estimated, estimation) the value of the jewelry to be nearly a million dollars.
5. If you are not satisfied with our product, we will (refund, refunding, refound)
   your money.
6. How many (itemize, items) do you have on your list?
7. Her secretary (mis-filing, mis-filed) the report in the wrong (file, filing).
8. We are (exemptions, exempt) from U.S. taxes because we live in Switzerland.
9. The store (gross, grossed) over $100,000 in revenues last year, but
   after all the expenses were paid, the owners (net, netted) only $10,000.
10. Mr. Thriftbottom wants to change his (will, wills) again because he doesn't want his
    youngest son to (inheritance, inherit) a penny.

B. Use the key words above in the following sentences. Use each word only once.

1. _____ income is larger than _____ income.
2. He bought a new _____.
3. In our company, the sales people get a _____ of the net sales.
4. In her _____ , she left her art collection to her daughter.
   Her son_____ the house.
5. If you over-pay your taxes, you'll get a _____.
6. My employer is_____ too much from my paycheck.
7. The consultant made an_____ that the company's revenues
   would decrease next year. In my estimation he's wrong.
8. After he re-checked all his _____, he discovered the error.
9. Will you _____ all your expenses, please. I need a complete list.
10. Can I _____ my tax forms late this year? I'll be out of the country on the due date.
11. She claimed three _____ , one for herself and one for each of her two children.

C. Use the correct form of each key word in these sentences.

1. (estimate) In my _____ his_____ is much too high.
2. (item) Last year I didn't _____ my deductions.
3. (refund) This year I think I will be _____ at least $500.
4. (inherit) Before he received the money, he had to pay an _____ tax.
5. (withhold) My _____ tax will total over $10,000 this year.
6. (percentage) In my estimation, 50 _____ is too high a
   _____ to pay.
7. (calculate) This cell phone can also do _____.
8. (compute) She wants to be a _____ programmer.
9. (file) This_____ system is very confusing. I don't know where to
   _____ the marketing report.
10. (will) In his _____, he _____ everything to his pet cat.
11. (net) The _____ result is, we have not made a profit.
12. (gross) Your _____ income, before taxes, is lower this year.
13. (exempt) To be _____ , you must have owed no federal income tax
    for the year.

D. Use one of the key words in each sentence.

1. I need a new battery for my _____.
2. The_____ of households owning two TVs has increased
   by 10% this year.
3. "Tear up my _____!" he shouted. "That rascal will never _____ any
   of my money."
4. "I'm sorry Mr. Jones, but we can't give you a _____ unless you have
   proof of purchase."
5. We think the government is _____ information, and we
   want the truth.
6. "How many _____ are there on the agenda for today's meeting?"
7. Because he is overweight he is _____ from military service.
8. Three different companies have submitted _____ for the cost of
   building the new bridge.
9. She's going to _____ a complaint against her landlord.
10. The movie *Star Wars* _____ millions of dollars at the box office, and
    _____ its producers a very nice profit.
11. According to Dr. Stargazer's _____, the new galaxy is a billion
    million light years away.

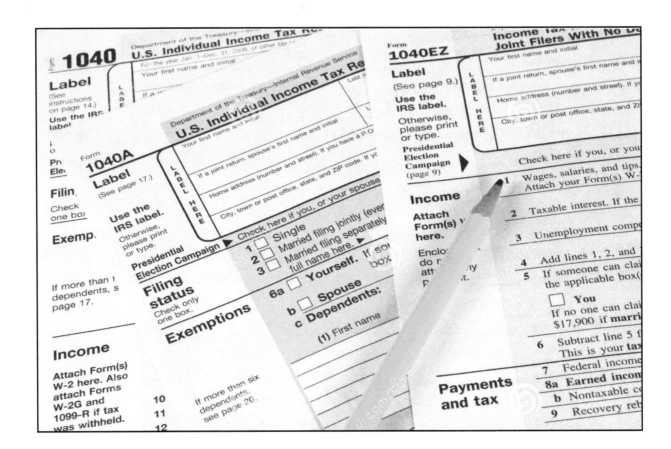

Talk About It

1. Is the U.S. federal tax system fair?

2. Which is better, an income tax or a sales tax?

3. Is an inheritance tax necessary?

4. When should we make a will?

Answers

1. An Introductory Reading

page 1

A
1. luxury, necessity
2. goods, services
3. use
4. useful
5. economics, economic, economist
6. needs
7. earns
8. The economy

B
1. banker
2. buyer
3. seller
4. user
5. earner
6. borrower
7. economist

2. Money: A Short History

page 3

A
1. valuable
2. supplies, commodities
3. Cashing, transaction
4. precious
5. worth
6. coinage, bills
7. currencies
8. payment
9. minted, mint

B
1. worth
2. precious
3. Coins, bills
4. cash
5. commodity
6. currency, value
7. transaction
8. payment
9. minted
10. supply

C
1. valuable, value
2. worthless
3. mint, supplied
4. commodities
5. pay, payments
6. transacted, transaction
7. cash, cashed

D
1. bill
2. mint
3. worth, value
4. Precious
5. commodity
6. cash, payment
7. currency, currencies
8. coin, coin
9. transaction
10. supplier, supplies

3. Using Money

page 8

A
1. spend
2. lend
3. loaning
4. borrowed
5. saved, purchased
6. invests, interest
7. Gambling, gambler, collecting, collector
8. Counterfeiting
9. exchange

B
1. spent, loan, borrow, lend, interest
2. exchanges, purchase, save, savings
3. investment, gamble
4. collection, counterfeit

C
1. loaned
2. borrowed
3. interest
4. purchased
5. spent
6. counterfeiter
7. collector, collects
8. gamble, savings
9. invested
10. exchange

D
1. collect, save, collection
2. exchange
3. counterfeiter, spend
4. invest, investment, loan
5. interest
6. gambling

4. Earning Money
page 13

A
1. capitalist
2. wealthy
3. contract
4. income
5. royalty
6. wages
7. employees, salary
8. fees
9. consult
10. raises
11. bonuses

B
1. royalties
2. contract
3. fee
4. wages
5. salary, income
6. capital
7. consultant
8. wealthy
9. employed
10. raise
11. bonus

C
1. salaries
2. wage
3. wealthy, income
4. consultant
5. employed
6. royalty
7. bonuses, raises
8. fees
9. capitalism

D
1. employs
2. Capital
3. salary
4. wage
5. royalties
6. consultant
7. fee
8. raise
9. contract
10. income
11. wealthy
12. bonus

5. Buying and Selling
page 18

A
1. deal, wholesale, bargain
2. market, promote
3. product, compete
4. retailers, profits
5. distributor
6. offer, bid
7. spend

B
1. retail
2. dealer, wholesale, consumers
3. profit, competitors
4. production, distribution, promotion
5. offer/bid
6. bid/offer
7. marketing
8. bargain

C
1. consumer
2. bidder
3. dealer
4. distributor
5. promoter
6. offerer
7. producer
8. wholesaler
9. retailer
10. competition
11. profit

D
1. offer
2. Market
3. produced
4. competing
5. (under)-bid
6. profits
7. consumer
8. dealer
9. distribution
10. bargaining, bargain
11. promotion, promote, promoted

6. Banks
page 22

A
1. bounce
2. funds
3. financial
4. reserve
5. balance, minimum
6. deposits, withdrawals
7. Commerce
8. trader, draws

B
1. deposit
2. withdraw
3. reserve
4. draw
5. statement, balance, minimum
6. funds
7. trade
8. commercial
9. Financial
10. bounced

C
1. reserves
2. deposited
3. withdrawal
4. balanced
5. minimum
6. statement
7. draw
8. funds
9. traded
10. financial
11. commercial
12. bounced

D
1. minimum
2. bounce
3. deposited
4. Fund
5. withdraw
6. draw
7. financial
8. statement
9. reserves/reserve
10. commercial
11. trade

7. Borrowing and Lending

page 26

A
1. owed, repaid
2. term, mortgage, principal, payments, deed, own
3. defaulted, risk, credit
4. debtor, sum, collateral

B
1. term
2. broke
3. deed
4. owe
5. own
6. debt
7. default
8. repay
9. risk
10. credit
11. collatural, principal, mortgage
12. sum

C
1. repaid
2. owe
3. deed, deeds
4. broke
5. debts
6. (long-)term
7. mortgaged
8. owner, collateral
9. sum
10. risked
11. creditors/creditor
12. defaulted

D
1. owe, broke, repaid
2. mortgage, deed, own
3. (short-) term
4. debt, risked
5. sum, credit
6. defaulted, principal

8. Plastic Money

page 30

A
1. stole
2. charge
3. accept
4. sales
5. unlimited
6. cost
7. rented
8. amounted, debit
9. transferred
10. rating

B
1. accept
2. rent
3. transfer
4. cost, down payment, installment
5. stolen, amount
6. charge, rating, limit
7. sales
8. debit card

C
1. rent
2. accepting, debit
3. installments
4. transferred
5. cost
6. stolen
7. charge
8. Sale
9. limit
10. amount
11. payments

D
1. transfer
2. down payment
3. accept
4. amount
5. limit
6. sales
7. stolen
8. charge, debit/credit
9. renting, costs, rating
10. installment

9. Investing

page 34

A
1. dividend
2. gainers
3. broker, trend
4. price
5. expensive
6. cheaper
7. issued, yielded
8. security
9. Real estate
10. shares, safe

B
1. cheap, expensive
2. price, gain
3. securities, safe
4. broker, shares
5. yield
6. dividend
7. issues
8. real estate
9. trend

C
1. expensive, cheapest
2. (highest-) priced
3. security
4. shares
5. safest
6. Brokers
7. gained
8. trend
9. (re-)issue
10. Dividends
11. yield
12. real estate

D
1. safe
2. broker
3. gain
4. expensive, cheap
5. price
6. trend, real estate
7. issued
8. dividend
9. share (holder)
10. Securities
11. yield

10. Budgeting and Accounting

page 38

A
1. deficit, revenues
2. fiscal
3. allowance
4. forecaster
5. expenses
6. accountant, accounts
7. Assets, liabilities, equity
8. counted
9. entity, non-entity
10. bottom line

B
1. expense
2. revenue
3. deficit
4. liability
5. asset
6. equity
7. bottom line
8. count
9. entities
10. allowance
11. fiscal
12. forecast
13. account

C
1. deficit
2. liabilities
3. allowed
4. account
5. counting
6. revenues/revenue
7. fiscally
8. Forecasting
9. expenses
10. entities
11. assets, equity, bottom line

D
1. forecast
2. allowance
3. bottom line
4. deficit
5. Revenue
6. fiscally, fiscal
7. assets
8. liabilities, equity
9. count
10. (non)-entity
11. expenses
12. account

11. Insurance

page 42

A
1. pensioner
2. beneficiary
3. disabled
4. deduction
5. policyholder
6. covered
7. protected
8. compensated
9. sues
10. disastrous
11. compulsory
12. premiums

B
1. pension
2. compulsory
3. policy, protection
4. disaster
5. disability
6. beneficiary
7. premium, coverage
8. sue
9. deductible
10. compensation

C
1. policies
2. beneficiaries
3. coverage, premiums
4. compensated
5. protected, pension
6. disabled
7. deducting
8. disastrous
9. sued
10. compulsory

D
1. policy/coverage
2. disasters
3. protect
4. beneficiary
5. premium
6. sue
7. pension, deducts, compulsory
8. disabled
9. compensated
10. coverage

12. Gambling

page 47

A
1. Betting
2. winner
3. illegal
4. luckily
5. hugest
6. passed
7. fold
8. favorite
9. odds
10. chance
11. fortunate
12. staking
13. wager

B
1. bet/wager
2. huge
3. stakes
4. odds
5. chance
6. won
7. favorite
8. pass
9. fortune
10. wagered/bet
11. folded
12. legalizing
13. unlucky

C
1. bet, bets
2. folded
3. winnings
4. staked
5. (un)fortunate
6. legalized
7. wager/bet
8. huge
9. odds
10. favorite, favoritism
11. lucky, luck
12. passes
13. chances

D
1. stakes
2. odds
3. chance
4. pass
5. huge
6. winning
7. fortune
8. folds
9. wager/bet
10. lucky
11. favorite
12. illegally
13. bet, bet

13. Changing Money

page 51

A
1. change
2. exported, imported
3. convert
4. flow
5. officially
6. stability
7. inflationary
8. Speculation
9. floating
10. monetary

B
1. exports, imports
2. official
3. Monetary
4. change
5. flow
6. volume
7. convert
8. denomination
9. Inflation
10. float
11. stable
12. speculate

C
1. importer, exporter
2. converted
3. change
4. denomination
5. official, officially, official
6. stability
7. monetary
8. Inflation
9. floated/floating, floating
10. Speculators
11. flow, volume

D
1. change
2. converted, speculation
3. exported, imports
4. official
5. inflation
6. monetary
7. denominations
8. stable
9. floating
10. volume
11. flowing

🏛 73 🏛

14. Money and Crime

page 56

A
1. merchants
2. Piracy
3. evade
4. fined
5. thieves
6. robbery, committed
7. fraud, cheating
8. embezzled
9. money launderer
10. Corruption
11. penalty

B
1. merchant
2. pirate
3. audited, evasion, penalty, fine
4. money laundering
5. robbed, thieves
6. committed
7. fraud, cheat
8. embezzle
9. corruption

C
1. merchant, merchandise
2. pirates
3. evasion
4. fined
5. thieves
6. committed
7. embezzled
8. money launderer
9. corrupt
10. fraud
11. cheating
12. auditor
13. penalty
14. robbed

D
1. merchandise
2. pirates, rob
3. evaded
4. money launderers/ing
5. commit
6. embezzled
7. cheating
8. corrupted
9. audit
10. fraud
11. penalty, fine
12. theft

15. Money and the Internet

page 60

A
1. wallet
2. online
3. scam
4. manage
5. ID thieves
6. advertisements
7. spam
8. subscriber
9. obsolete
10. lucrative
11. website
12. expiration, code

B
1. online
2. manager
3. websites
4. spam
5. subscribes
6. advertising
7. obsolete
8. ID theft
9. wallet
10. expiration
11. code
12. lucrative scam

C
1. subscription, expire
2. online , website
3. spam, scam
4. lucrative
5. code, ID theft
6. advertising manager
7. wallets
8. obsolete

D
1. manage, online
2. website, lucrative
3. scam
4. subscribe
5. expiration, code
6. ID theft
7. spam, advertising
8. obsolete

16. Death and Taxes

page 64

A
1. withheld
2. computer, calculations
3. percent
4. estimated
5. refund
6. items
7. mis-filed, file
8. exempt
9. grossed, netted
10. will, inherit

B
1. Gross, net
2. calculator
3. percentage
4. will, inherited
5. refund
6. withholding
7. estimate
8. computations
9. itemize
10. file
11. exemptions

C
1. estimation, estimate
2. itemize
3. refunded
4. inheritance
5. withholding
6. percent,percentage
7. calculations/calculation
8. computer
9. filing, file
10. will, willed
11. net
12. gross
13. exempt

D
1. calculator
2. percentage
3. will, inherit
4. refund
5. withholding
6. items
7. exempt
8. estimates
9. file
10. grossed, netted
11. computations

APPENDICES

1. Milestones in the World of Money

2. Wages and Salaries

3. The 25 Most Traded Currencies

1. Milestones in the World of Money

640	B.C.E.	First true coins developed by Lydians.
560-546	B.C.E.	Croesus creates the world's first official government coinage.
600s	C.E.	Paper money in use in China.
1100s	C.E.	Development of banks in Italy (The name bank comes from the Latin *bancus*, "bench.")
1689	C.E.	Lloyd's of London issues the first insurance policy.
1690	C.E.	First paper money in the U.S. issued by Massachusetts Bay Colony.
1694	C.E.	Bank of England established.
1792	C.E.	U.S. dollar and the national mint in Philadelphia established.
1913	C.E.	U.S. Federal Reserve System created.
1929	C.E.	The Great Stock Market Crash.
1944	C.E.	Bretton Woods Conference resulting in establishment of the International Monetary Fund (IMF) and the World Bank.
2002	C.E.	Thirteen European nations introduce Euro coins and banknotes.

2. Wages and Salaries

How much money do people earn in various occupations? It depends on many things: how long they have worked at their job, how skilled they are, how much education they have, and even though it may be illegal, whether they are a man or a woman. It also depends on the place where they live. In New York City, where the cost of living is very high, a bus driver may make more money than a bus driver with similar qualifications who lives in a small town.

The figures below are from the U.S. Department of Labor (2017 data). They represent the average for the entire country. Therefore it is likely that a skilled bus driver in New York City earns more than $35,000.

Fast Food Worker	$21,400
Store Cashier	22,160
Bank Teller	22,800
Child Care Worker	23,760
Farmworker	25,070
Waiter	25,280
Cook	25,440
Baker	27,900
Bus Driver	35,000
Auto Mechanic	45,600
Carpenter	49,630
Post Office Worker	50,160
Plumber	57,070
Elementary School Teacher	60,800
Police Officer	64,540
Registered Nurse	73,550
Electrical Engineer	102,600
Software Developer	111,780
Economist	112,650
Lawyer	139,900
Airplane Pilot	161,280
Chief Executive Officer	196,050

3. The 25 Most Traded Currencies

(from Countries-of-the-World.com 9/20/2018)

Rank	Currency	Code: Share of Daily Trade *	Country or Territory
1	US dollar	USD: 87.62	United States
2	European euro	EUR: 31.27	19 States of the EU
3	Japanese yen	JPY: 21.56	Japan
4	Pound sterling	GBP: 12.78	United Kingdom of Great Britain
5	Australian dollar	AUD: 6.94	Australia
6	Canadian dollar	CAD: 5.13	Canada
7	Swiss franc	CHF: 4.78	Switzerland
8	Chinese Yuan Renminbi	CNY: 3.97	China
9	Swedish krona	SEK: 2.22	Sweden
10	Mexican peso	MXN: 2.20	Mexico
11	New Zealand dollar	NZD: 2.06	New Zealand
12	Singapore dollar	SGD: 1.79	Singapore
13	Hong Kong dollar	HKD: 1.73	Hong Kong
14	Norwegian krone	NOK: 1.67	Norway
15	South Korean won	KRW: 1.65	South Korea
16	Turkish lira	TRY: 1.40	Turkey
17	Indian rupee	INR: 1.14	India
18	Russian ruble	RUB: 1.14	Russia
19	Brazilian real	BRL 1.00	Brazil
20	South African rand	ZAR: 1.00	South Africa
21	Danish krone	DKK: 0.83	Denmark
22	Polish zloty	PLN: 0.69	Poland
23	New Taiwan dollar	TWD: 0.63	Taiwan
24	Thai baht	THB: 0.43	Thailand
25	Malaysian ringgit	MYR: 0.41	Malaysia

* Share of 200 total

Key Word Index

(Numbers are Unit Numbers)

OTHER VOCABULARY DEVELOPMENT BOOKS

American Holidays.* 20 units/holidays. 195 words exploring traditions, customs, and backgrounds of the holidays. Audio CD available.

Potluck. Exploring North American Meals, Culinary Practices, and Places. 24 Units. 288 key words. 2 audio CDs available.

Wheels and Wings. 143 key words associated with the world of transportation and travel.

The Zodiac The Vocabulary of Human Qualities and Characteristics. Audio CD available.

Shopping (under development)

OTHER BOOKS ON VOCABULARY

Lexicarry.* Pictures for Learning Languages. Over 4500 everyday words and expressions. Word lists in twelve languages correlated with the drawings.

Getting a Fix on Vocabulary: A student text that focuses on affixation. Includes all the common prefixes and suffixes and the most common bases. Text also includes "radio news" on audio CD.

The Learner's Lexicon. A word frequency list of 2400 words, divided into 300-, 600-, 1200-, and 2400-word lists.

Got It! Vocabulary games where teams compete to come up with words that are associated with lexical sets – work, food, body, weather, etc.

Go Fish. Seven beginning-level card games that focus on the basic vocabulary of the home (86 words).

Coloring in English. Beginning-level vocabulary-building coloring book for kids and adults. 40 pictures; 400 words.

A-Z Picture Activities.* Phonics and Vocabulary for Emerging Readers. One unit for each letter of the alphabet. Dozens of pictures. Audio CD available.

The Idiom Book.* 1001 Idioms in Two-Page Lessons. Based on everyday events. 2 audio CDs available.

A Phrasal Verb Affair.* 250 phrasal verbs from "add up to" to "zero in on" in a soap opera of 15 episodes. Audio CD available.

*Available as eBook/digital editions

ProLinguaAssociates.com